CU00404920

i

First Edition June 2017

THE MODERN BRITISH

SLAVERY SYSTEM

by

Gerard Atherton

2017

Edited by Erik Kowal

iv

CONTENTS

Author's Preface

The scope of this book is limited to Britain (meaning the United Kingdom of Great Britain and Northern Ireland), since that is where I have lived and worked for most of my 60 years. I have some understanding of its laws and systems, and so I feel confident in writing about them. However, similar systems of slavery exist in most of the rest of the world to a greater or lesser extent. It is easy to spot a country that operates under slavery. If wages are so low that a legal minimum wage must be introduced to lift people above subsistence level wages, there is almost certainly a slavery system in operation that is forcing wages down.

I have tried to refrain from analysing history and describing how we arrived at the current British system of slavery, but I do occasionally refer to the past for relevant examples. I will leave the analysis of history to the historians, in order to focus on the situation we find ourselves in now.

In recent years I have come to understand more fully the nature of this system of slavery, and I've found it very demoralising. I am sure that a similar degree of demoralisation is present throughout Britain's workforce, and can only imagine how much more enriching and rewarding life would be if this system was replaced with something more civilized.

I feel that it's impossible to say anything sensible about almost any topic in Britain without first understanding how wealth is distributed by its iniquitous slavery system. The distortions it has introduced make it difficult to say anything rational about politics, education, welfare, etc. Almost anything one hears in the media, especially from politicians, is full of contradictions and confusion. This and a sense of fairness are what have motivated me to write this book.

I don't blame anybody for the system we find ourselves in. We are all caught in it and doing our best within it. Which of us would not act similarly if we were born into a different walk of life?

I hope that one day, the private ownership of land will be viewed in the same way that we now view the private ownership of human beings. This book will demonstrate that they are effectively the same thing.

I first came across the notion of charging rent for land at the age of 25, when I attended a series of ten ninety-minute economics talks at the School of Economic Science in London. These few hours completely changed my worldview. In fact, I don't think I *had* a worldview before then, or indeed any coherent understanding of the world. I was merely progressing through life, taking advantage of whatever opportunities arose. But since then I have been looking at the world through the prism of that idea of charging rent for land, and trying to make sense of the current system of wealth distribution.

I also realised that other people had been thinking about the same subject. Henry George, a 19th-century American economist, wrote a book called *Progress and Poverty*. He tried to explain why, with so much progress being made in the creation of wealth using the new technologies developed during the Industrial Revolution, there was still so much poverty. He attempted to show that the unfair distribution of wealth was due to the system of private ownership of land. Other notable writers on the subject were David Ricardo and Adam Smith. I was also influenced by Kevin Cahill's book *Who Owns Britain*, which reveals how concentrated the private ownership of land is in Britain.

To eliminate the current system of slavery, all that is necessary is to do away with the system of control that allows people to be enslaved – namely, the private ownership of land by a minority. Marx required us all to be as unselfish as angels, whereas land rent requires only a change to the tax system.

Most of my working life was spent as a business analyst working to implement new information technology systems in businesses. The standard approach to implementing a new system is to first understand, document and analyse the existing system and the problems it causes, and then to propose and document a new system to solve those problems. I have organised this book in a similar way. Sections one to four deal with the existing system. Section five describes possible solutions, and section six focuses on the proposed solution.

Acknowledgements

I am deeply grateful to my partner, Dr. Christine Ziehmann, for supporting and encouraging me in writing this book.

I would also like to thank Erik Kowal who edited the book, and gave me encouragement when I needed it most.

1 Comparing the Modern British and Caribbean Slavery Systems

1.1 Introduction

It is common knowledge that there exist extremes of wealth distribution in Britain. We regularly read reports in the media about how a small percentage of the population owns a very high percentage of the country's wealth. According to a recent report from Oxfam[1], the richest 1% of the UK population owns more than 20 times the wealth of the poorest 20%.It seems that Britain is very good at producing wealth, but not so good at distributing it fairly.

There's a famous patriotic song whose chorus goes:

> "Rule, Britannia! Britannia, rule the waves!
> Britons never, never, never shall be slaves."

Unfortunately for most Britons, that is exactly what they are – slaves. The principal reason for the unfair distribution of wealth in Britain is that the British economy is based on a system of slavery. A small percentage of private individuals and organisations have stolen the land, and with the assistance of four groups of well-paid accomplices, they are extracting for themselves an unearned proportion of the wealth produced by the slaves who must work on this land.

Data published by Her Majesty's Revenue and Customs (HMRC) shows that there is a problem.

1 Comparing the Modern British and Caribbean Slavery Systems

In 2014-15, the median wage was £22,400, but the mean wage was £31,800[2]. This shows that the receipt of wages is skewed towards a small number of individuals who are earning much more than everyone else. This is just what we would expect to see in a slave society in which the poor are abnormally poor and the rich are abnormally rich.

As for the ownership of assets, we can look at the HMRC's data for unearned income. This is income that comes from the ownership of assets such as property which earns (or more accurately, un-earns) rent, dividend-earning shares in companies, and debt that earns interest. The recipients of this income have not had to do any work to obtain this income; they have merely had to own assets, hence the term 'unearned income'. The owners of these assets are taking the wealth that others have produced.

Unearned income must be declared separately from earned income on tax returns. In the tax year 2013-2014, £951 billion[3] was declared for tax (though there may be a lot of unearned income in tax havens that wasn't declared), of which unearned income comprised £81.6 billion. Twenty-six million people received some form of unearned income. According to data obtained from HMRC, the mean unearned income was £3190[4], but the median amount was only £45, which indicates that the majority of this unearned income was going to a tiny minority of people. This means that the ownership of the assets from which this unearned income is derived is heavily skewed to a minority of Britain's population.

This is confirmed by looking at the breakdown. Only 1.8 million people received income from property, and only 4.6 million people received income from dividends. This further confirms that the large majority of income-generating assets (such as property and shares) belong to a small percentage of the population, which again is precisely what one would expect in a slave society.

This book explains how this Modern British Slavery System (hereafter abbreviated to MBSS) operates, and how it impacts most aspects of our lives and culture. It dispels the widely-believed myth that the distribution of wealth in Britain is based purely on merit. The book will show that it is actually primarily based on (often inherited) land ownership, which leads directly to slavery.

1.2 Slavery systems

A system of slavery is characterised by individuals or organisations having some form of control over other people (i.e. slaves) that enables them to keep some or even most of the wealth that the slaves produce, producing consequent distortions in the distribution of wealth. This system results in the slave owners becoming abnormally wealthy, and the slaves becoming abnormally poor.

Work is required to produce from the earth wealth in all its myriad forms, such as food, drink, clothing, shelter, fuel, electronic goods etc. The objective of the slave owners is to enjoy this wealth without working themselves.

Some people think slavery can only be rightly called slavery if people are being whipped, or if families are separated and sold to the highest bidder in a slave market; but cruel phenomena of this kind are merely markers of the possession of absolute control over other people. The main characteristic of slavery is forced work, plus the slave owners' ability to acquire some or most of the wealth that the slaves produce. Though the slaves produce wealth, their wages are less than the true value of the wealth they have produced, with the difference being pocketed by those who have control over the slaves.

Other people may prefer to call the MBSS 'controlled labour'. To me this is just a euphemism for something much worse. Having the control to extract the wealth that others have produced *is* slavery, pure and simple.

1.3 The Caribbean system of slavery

For a slavery system to function, I suggest there are three key factors that have to be present. Using the Caribbean sugar plantation system of slavery as an example, in section 1.4 I will show how these same three factors are present in the MBSS.

1.3.1 Control over people

In the slavery system that existed on the Caribbean sugar plantations, the method of control was established by laws that allowed people to own other people – slaves, in other words. The plantation owners owned not only the land of the plantation but also the people on it. If the slaves hadn't been owned they might have preferred to escape and fend for themselves on some uninhabited land, which there was then plenty of in this New World. Chaining them could prevent them from easily escaping, but even if they did escape they could be legally hunted down by the authorities and returned to their 'rightful' owner. A brand on the body of the slave could identify the owner.

The slaves were forcibly abducted into this system of law, became the legal property of slave owners, and were then set to work on plantations. The plantation owners retained most of the profits produced by their slaves, merely forfeiting to them some expenditure on minimal food, clothing and accommodation. Work was enforced through all sorts of cruel measures. If the slaves revolted, a law enforcement agency like the army would be called in to quell the rebellion.

1.3.2   Accomplices

The plantation owners could not have achieved this theft of wealth from the slaves without the assistance of a few groups of accomplices; and the accomplices would not have assisted in this theft without being rewarded with a portion of the wealth stolen from the slaves. The size of their reward would depend on the degree to which they helped in the process of extracting wealth from the slaves. Each group of accomplices incorporated a hierarchy of status and corresponding rewards without which the system would not have been able to function.

The first two groups of accomplices were part of the state apparatus. One was the lawmakers who set up the laws that permitted the ownership of people. Although slavery in England had been banned since the signing of the Magna Carta in 1215, the authorities on these British-owned islands in the Caribbean developed 'slave codes' in the seventeenth century which legitimized the ownership of people on the grounds that they were uncivilised and not Christian.

The second group of accomplices consisted of the enforcers of the laws that the lawmakers had created, ranging from local law officers to the army. The degree of involvement of a given type of law enforcer would depend on the extent of the slave rebellion.

These first two groups of accomplices established and enforced the framework of a system which the third group of accomplices could then exploit on behalf of the plantation/slave owners. This third group consisted of the slave managers, overseers and slave drivers who operated on behalf of the plantation/slave owners. Their role was to manage the slaves and, within the laws set down by the lawmakers, to 'motivate' the slaves to work as hard and efficiently as possible. The lawmakers defined the degree of cruelty permissible for such 'motivation', and we all have some understanding of what that involved.

The plantation owners took the wealth that the slaves produced, rewarded their accomplices with some of the proceeds, and gave as little as possible to the slaves. The minimum wealth that the slaves needed to keep body and soul together comprised their rations of food and drink, clothing (typically one new set per year), shelter, and perhaps just enough health care to enable them to stay productive. The system clearly allowed these 'wages' to be reduced to the minimum required to keep the slaves working efficiently.

Owning slaves is a constant balancing act. The slave owners had to keep asking themselves how far they could push the slaves to make them work as long and hard as possible for as little reward as possible without triggering a rebellion. This balancing act was made especially dangerous by the fact that the slaves usually far outnumbered their owners and accomplices. The most successful rebellion of slaves in history occurred in Haiti, where it led to the founding of a state freed from slavery.

1.3.3 Meritocracy within the slave ranks

Even in a slavery system, it benefited the plantation owners to institute a degree of meritocracy that permitted slaves to be rewarded extra if they either improved the wealth creation process or helped to manage the process of extracting wealth from the other slaves.

If a slave took on a more highly skilled role on the plantation, such as that of a carpenter, they could receive a higher 'wage' in the form of reduced field work and beatings, or additional privileges and rations. The slave owner got the benefit of their skilled work with little extra cost.

Note that the extra skill, in the case of a carpenter, consists in designing and building capital. Capital is defined in greater detail in section 2.1.10, but is essentially human-created material that is designed not to be consumed immediately but is intended to last and make the production of wealth more efficient. The carpenter produced buildings, structures such as ditch supports, and tools that would allow the other slaves on the plantation to work more efficiently. The results of the carpenter's work – the capital – became the property of the plantation owner.

Likewise, if a slave rose to be a slave driver – in other words, an accomplice – they would also be compensated with higher 'wages' in the form of privileges and sometimes monetary rewards. The slave driver's position was a difficult one. To maintain the goodwill of the owners by implementing their harsh regime without losing the respect of their fellow-slaves was no small achievement. (Modern-day low-level managers may recognise how this feels.)

Another important benefit for the owners from instituting an element of meritocracy in their slavery system was that it encouraged their slaves to compete with each other, distracting their attention from their overall plight.

A slave born into and raised in slavery might not have known anything better, and everything might have seemed perfectly normal. They worked hard at cultivating and harvesting sugar most days, but had little understanding of what happened to it afterwards. In return for their work they received food, clothes and shelter. If they worked harder than their fellow slaves and developed their skills, they might earn some extra privileges or food that would make life seem better. They might not have perceived that the system of meritocracy was just one component embedded in a much bigger system of slavery in which much of the distribution of the sugar wealth was hidden from their observation and understanding.

The owners of these plantations were no respecters of whatever natural, close and supportive relationships might have developed among the slaves living there. Husbands and wives, children, brothers and sisters, grandparents, friends – all these relationships were subordinate to the production of wealth. It is possible to read many accounts of slaves being sold to another plantation far away when it suited the plantation owner.

The solution to the Caribbean slavery system was a law passed in 1833 that made the ownership of other people illegal. Once this legal control over people was removed, the slaves were then theoretically free to establish themselves on unoccupied land. Unfortunately, by then most of the land in the New World was already owned by other people. So the slaves were merely shifted into a more benign system of slavery that was similar to the system which exists in Britain today, but was characterised by more extensive racial prejudice.

1.4 Parallels in the Modern British Slavery System

This section gives an overview of how the current system of wealth distribution in Britain is based on a system of slavery that, although less cruel, has very close parallels with the Caribbean system described in the previous section. The same three factors that were present in the Caribbean system are also present in the MBSS:

1.4.1 Control over people

The MBSS is much subtler than the Caribbean system (in fact, it is so subtle that few people realise that it is a system of slavery) in permitting a group of owners and their accomplices to become abnormally rich, and their slaves to become abnormally poor.

In the Caribbean slaves were legally owned, so it was pretty clear who was a slave and who was not. One of the things that makes the MBSS less visible and thus more subtle than the Caribbean system is that it creates no obvious boundary line between slaves and non-slaves. There is no legal status of slave. People cannot be owned. They have a right to their liberty, and the right not to be subjected to physical assault.

In Britain, control over people is achieved not through the ownership of people, but through the ownership of the thing that everyone needs in order to live – *land*. A small minority own the freehold of most of the commercial land, i.e. the land on which businesses operate. People need access to land for their survival, in the same way that they cannot survive without air and sunshine. They need land in order to grow food, build houses, manufacture cars etc. If landowners own most of the available commercial land, they have control of the people that need to work on it, and this gives them the power to extract wealth from them. The people are thus enslaved: in order to be able to work for a living, they are subtly forced to hand over some of the wealth they create to the landowners and their accomplices. The mechanism by which this happens will be explained in more detail in section 2.

What exacerbates the problem is the fact that the minority who own the land do so on a freehold basis. They own the land, and they pay no financial penalty for keeping it out of use, or for reserving large plots of land simply for their sporting pastimes. This gives them the opportunity to maintain a scarcity of available land for a growing population. As a result, rents are forced higher, correspondingly subtracting from the effective purchasing power of the wages earned. Wages consequently bear no relationship to the value of the goods that the workers are producing. The landowners and their accomplices sell the goods at their true value, pay the workers their slave wages, and pocket the difference.

Unlike the case of the New World of the 17th century, where escaped slaves could flee to unowned land, all the land in Britain is now somebody's property. Although the British notionally have their liberty, it doesn't much benefit them because there is no free land to run to. Wherever they might wish to escape to, the same slavery conditions exist.

1.4.2 Accomplices

The MBSS needs accomplices, just as the Caribbean system did. These accomplices belong to groups similar to those found in the Caribbean system – lawmakers, law enforcers and managers. However, there is a unique fourth accomplice that is essential to the more subtle UK system of slavery – the Bank of England, as I explain in more detail in section 2. Besides the Bank of England, I also include bankers and the finance industry as a whole in this category of accomplices.

The accomplices are key components in the system of slavery, but I suspect that most of them have no understanding of their role in this crime. They are merely doing their jobs, and are unable to see how their activities fit into the wider system. I'm sure many of these individuals try to be just, but they are operating within the confines of a hidden slavery system which is inherently unjust.

1.4.3 Meritocracy within the slave ranks

The MBSS encompasses a greater degree of meritocracy within the slave ranks than existed in the Caribbean system, so that most people are fooled into believing that we live in a pure meritocracy. They do not see that the meritocratic system is merely an embedded component in a wider system of slavery, just as it was in the Caribbean. This belief often coincides with what they would wish to be true, especially if they are doing relatively well within the slave meritocracy.

Most workers never realize that they are slaves, handing over the wealth they produce to the rich minority and their accomplices. The reason for this is that the forgone wealth doesn't come directly out of their pay packets. The wealth they create is handed over to the landowners by the businesses they work for, long before the money received in exchange for that wealth reaches their own pay packets. The distribution of the wealth that the slave has made is thereby concealed, both by being obscured from view and by virtue of its complexity. There is more to it than this, as I will explain in section 2.5.

Under this system, a large number of people can be reduced to receiving subsistence wages – in other words, to slavery – while a few accomplices receive higher wages for assisting the landowners with their unjust practice of extracting wealth from their slaves.

Today's slaves have more wealth at their disposal than the former slaves of the Caribbean. Our ability to generate wealth has increased massively. Besides getting enough food, clothes and shelter, today's slaves may benefit from some electronic goods and a bit of travel. However, the wealth of today's slaves pales into insignificance compared to the wealth of today's landowners, with the disparity in many cases being even greater than existed in the Caribbean.

Just as the system that operated in the Caribbean was no respecter of natural human relationships, neither is the MBSS. No sooner have children grown up than they are scattered across the globe, lured by dreams of wealth. These naive adults find a mate and raise their own small family, only to see their children too get scattered across the globe. Perhaps some children are only too happy to escape their families, especially if those families are attempting to impose dogmatic religious or political views on them. But the end result is that we are left with a lot of lonely, isolated people who have little social support.

1 Comparing the Modern British and Caribbean Slavery Systems

2 The Operation of the Modern British Slavery System

Section 1 showed that we live in a subtle system of slavery that has close parallels with the former Caribbean slavery system. Section 2 will describe in greater detail how the MBSS operates.

2.1 Elements of the MBSS

To understand the MBSS more fully, we need to define and understand its main elements.

2.1.1 Land

This book uses the term 'land' as a shorthand way of referring to any natural resource – in other words, anything useful that is not created by humans. For example, its referents include all of the following: agricultural land, moorland, land under houses, land under businesses, parkland, forests, mineral deposits such as oil, coal, ores of iron and copper etc, lakes, rivers, the air, the airwaves and sunshine.

'Land' does not include anything which humans have made by using the land, such as clothes, buildings, houses, furniture, food and drink, cars – the list is endless. These are all things where humans, driven by their desires, have taken something that is naturally-occurring and have done some work on it to create 'wealth' which is then either consumed or is sold to or rented to somebody else.

There are potentially fuzzy areas of definition, like land reclaimed from the sea. Some might say that such

15

reclaimed land is human-made. However, this is more of a reconfiguration of land than a product of wealth creation. Some of the sea has been 'destroyed' and land has been 'created'. Fish can no longer swim where the sea once was.

2.1.2   Land value

The value of land depends on many factors, but in this section of the book I will discuss only one of them – supply and demand. I will address the others in section 3.6.

In Britain, the supply of the urban land that its growing population needs is kept perpetually scarce. Landowners who own the freehold of green-belt land around Britain's cities, towns and villages dribble it into the market at the highest price. Under the freehold system of land tenure, there is no financial penalty for withholding undeveloped land from production.

Some people consider that the rent paid for, say, a high-street shop must be a fair one because we have a competition-based free market which ensures that it will be so. (Most businesses rent their premises – they cannot afford to buy the freehold, and it is not normally for sale in any case.) They believe that if the prospective renter considers the proposed rent too expensive they can always try the next site down the high street, and that this mechanism of competition will keep the rents as low as possible.

This perception is mistaken. Under the freehold system, there is no penalty for owning land and keeping it out of production. So landowners are able to operate a land-scarcity policy without penalty. If land is in short supply, so that there are always more people wanting to rent land than there is land available, there will be scarcity, and the price of land and rents will rise to the maximum that the site can support, at the expense of wages. The landowner doesn't care if a retailer declines their offered rent – a rent that is priced to minimise wages – because there will be another retailer along later in the day, and another, and one of them will eventually accept their terms. (The same is true of house prices. Housing land is deliberately kept in short supply so that the price that people pay is always pushed to the maximum they can afford.)

If the population was falling, such that there was a surplus of urban land, the people looking to rent shops or buy houses would have the upper hand, and in a free market they could force rents to the minimum that the landowner would accept. Wages would then rise correspondingly. Historians claim that this is exactly what happened in the aftermath of the decimation of the population by the Black Death: rents fell and wages rose.

However, in such a situation today, landowners would probably demolish buildings and take land out of production at a rate that kept rents as high as possible.

There is a recent example of the lengths landowners will go to in order to keep their land out of production. Business rate taxes used not to apply to unused commercial buildings. In 2008, Gordon Brown proposed levying rates for empty buildings[5] (but not for empty plots of land); owners who could not, or did not, want to pay the tax then simply demolished their buildings.

2.1.3   Land ownership

The land was here long before humans arrived. It does not make sense for individuals or organisations to be able to claim that land belongs to them, and that they owe nothing to society as a consequence of claiming it for themselves. Unfortunately, over time land has been appropriated by a minority. In some cases this was done by force, and in others with the assistance of accomplices, such as with the Acts of Enclosure. The result is that there is now little or no commercial land that people have access to without paying rent to a landowner.

Some people consider that removing their right to own land rent-free is tantamount to taking away their liberty. What these people don't consider is that on this crowded planet, taking land deprives others of *their* liberty. They are in fact enslaving those who do not own land.

In Britain, all land is nominally owned by the Crown. The Crown allows people to occupy most land on a freehold basis in which the freeholder does not have to pay any rent or service to the Crown and is free to sell it to another freeholder. Freeholders of land are also free to let it out for rent or to lease it out, which is essentially a form of long-term renting.

Anyone who doubts that the majority of the freeholds of commercial land are owned by a small minority of individuals and organisations should read *Who Owns Britain* by Kevin Cahill. As Mr Cahill explains, the land was stolen in three major land grabs, namely during the Norman Conquest, the dissolution of the monasteries, and the Civil War. I would add the Acts of Enclosure, whereby

Parliament passed more than 5,000 Acts[6] that transferred land from common ownership to private ownership.

In Britain today, the 10 largest landowners by area are[7]:

1. the Forestry Commission. Owned by the state. 2.5 million acres,
2. the National Trust. Charity. 630,000 acres,
3. the Ministry of Defence. Government department. 592,000 acres,
4. UK pension funds. 550,000 acres,
5. utilities. Various private and state-owned companies. 550,000 acres,
6. the Crown Estate. Owned by the monarch, run by the government. 358,000 acres,
7. the RSPB. Charity. 321,000 acres,
8. the Duke of Buccleuch & Queensberry. Individual. 240,000 acres,
9. the National Trust for Scotland. Charity. 192,000 acres,
10. the Duke of Atholl. Individual. 146,000 acres.

There are approximately 60 million acres of land in Britain, and the list above accounts for about 10% of it. Who owns the rest? Housing only accounts for 5%[8], and only about 65% of that (and falling) is owner-occupied.

The fact is that the rest is owned by individuals and organisations that represent a very small percentage of the population. The amount owned by each person/organisation in this minority ranges from those who own many acres, such as the above-mentioned Duke of Buccleuch & Queensberry with 240,000 acres, down to a person who might own their own house and maybe a buy-to-let house. The value of land also varies, ranging from moorland to high-value land such as the estate owned by the Duke of Westminster in parts of London (including Mayfair).

As can be seen from the above list, land is not only owned by individuals. In addition to the organisations listed above, the Church of England is still a big landowner. The colleges of Oxford and Cambridge were granted a lot of land when they were founded, and they still retain much of it to this day. The agricultural land they own does not bring in much rent, but the land they own in the centres of Oxford and Cambridge brings in huge rents.

As Kevin Cahill points out, the aristocracy are major landowners despite no longer having a direct role in the running of our society. Once, their power was almost limitless, but in a supposedly democratic society they are now an anachronism. The New Labour government effectively cut them off from direct political power by substantially reducing their numbers in the House of Lords. But we still have the hangover of their ownership of a lot of the land of Britain.

The aristocracy like to believe they are superior to other people, which is a very common way of justifying slavery. The slaves are considered to be inferior, and are thus available for exploitation. But in reality, the aristocracy are no better than anybody else. We see Julian Fellowes, the scriptwriter of the Downton Abbey TV series, trying to maintain this myth of superiority by putting words into Lord Grantham's mouth to make him appear prescient, such as when a new airplane was being discussed and Lord Grantham is made to say "I am sure that one day they will be flying all over the world". The reality is that anybody can create the appearance of superiority if they have a great deal of spare time and a lot of unearned money from rent that enables them to obtain the best education and pursue an interest in art and philosophy, fine wines, art, opera, horse racing, table manners etc.

One thing the writer of Downton Abbey doesn't show us is where the money comes from to maintain this family living their life of luxury in a splendid house. All we ever see is a single tenant farmer. Does the family live off the rent paid by him? Of course not. In real life, a Lord Grantham equivalent would own multiple commercial premises in our towns and cities from which he would draw sufficient rent to sustain the luxurious lifestyle enjoyed by him and his family. But the author does not want to show us this. The slaves might get too close to the truth.

A real-life equivalent of the Downton Abbey estate is exemplified by the Duchy of Cornwall. One might be forgiven for imagining that the land owned by the Duchy consists purely of farmland in Cornwall. In fact, the Duchy owns 18 commercial premises in London which are rented or leased to businesses, as well as 39 residential premises[9].

The aristocracy may be an anachronism, and they may have been largely cut off from the House of Lords, but they still own a lot of Britain's land. With the money from this they still wield power and influence, especially over their representatives in politics, the Conservative Party. Normally, we don't see this in action because it all takes place behind a curtain, but occasionally the curtain slips and we can observe the manipulation.

One example concerned the Cecil Rhodes statue that is displayed in Oxford High Street and owned by Oriel College. Rhodes was an 'empire-builder' in southern Africa. 'Empire-building' is a euphemism for 'land-grabbing on a massive scale', and Rhodes was therefore an enslaver. After the 'Rhodes must fall' campaign demanded that the statue be removed, Oriel College announced a structured six-month consultation on the subject of the statue, starting from early February 2016, to seek the views of all those involved. However, before the consultation had even started, the governing body of Oriel suddenly cancelled it and announced that the statue would remain. The reason for the reversal became clear when a leaked copy of a report prepared for the governors disclosed that wealthy alumni were threatening to write the college out of their wills if the statue was removed.

Here is another example: I used to take an interest in the annual reports published by the Land Registry. In 2006 only about 50% of UK land mass was registered[10]. Any land in Britain which is bought has to be registered for a small charge, but if it is inherited it does not have to undergo the registration process. Landowners do not like to register their land because they prefer to keep their ownership secret. Under the New Labour government the Land Registry increased its efforts to encourage voluntary registration of land for a discounted fee, setting itself an annual registration target of a certain number of hectares. Progress against this target was reported in the Land Registry's annual report. [11] Their major success was persuading Prince Charles to register the land of the Duchy of Cornwall. However, as soon as the Conservative Party came to power as the major partner in the 2010 coalition, the setting of voluntary land registration targets and the reporting on them was immediately and silently dropped. In the 2011-12 report[12] and all reports since then there is not a single mention of voluntary registrations. I have little doubt that this was due to the influence of landowners over the Conservative Party.

The freehold ownership of land does not encourage the efficient use of land. There is no penalty for owning land and leaving it idle. In fact, under the EU's Common Agricultural Policy's set-aside scheme, farmers can be paid for not using it. Not putting land to good use exacerbates the supply-and-demand problem described in section 1.4.1, thereby increasing the rent for surrounding land. Sites often stand idle for years in the centres of our towns and cities. There are reportedly hundreds of thousands of houses that are left permanently empty.

Freeholdism encourages land speculation. People can simply buy land and keep it out of use, in the full knowledge that a growing population, plus the development of new technology and automation, will force its value higher and higher, with no work being required by the owner. The house-building companies know this very well. They invest in huge land banks and wait for the value of the land to go up before they build their houses. A lot of their profits come simply from land speculation.

Rich land speculators buy newly-built houses and flats with no intention of using them. They leave them empty until they decide to sell them, knowing full well that the land they stand on will only increase in value, and without the hassle associated with letting.

2.1.4 Accomplices

It is one thing for a group of landowners to own most of Britain's commercial land, but another to get the millions of people on it to generate wealth and then hand over large portions of that wealth to the landowners. To assist them in this crime the landowners need certain accomplices, just as a sugar-plantation owner did. These accomplices are then overcompensated to greater or lesser degrees, depending on their contribution to the process of extracting wealth from the slaves.

The accomplices are key components of the slavery system, but I suspect that, on the whole, they have no understanding of their role in this moral crime. They are merely doing their job, and are not able to see how it fits into the wider system of slavery.

2.1.4.1 Lawmakers

By the term 'lawmakers' I primarily mean the MPs in the House of Commons who pass Acts of Parliament into law.

The landowners' first requirement of these lawmaking accomplices (historically, the landowners and the lawmakers were one and the same – and, to a lesser extent, they still are today) is for them to make the ownership of the stolen land legal by passing legitimising acts of Parliament, such as in the case of the 5000+ Acts of Enclosure passed in the period spanning the 17th to the 19th centuries. Under the freehold system the landowners can own and enjoy land, and have no responsibility to pay society for the privilege.

Today, most commercial land in Britain is privately owned, so the lawmakers have little to do in terms of allocating further land to the rich. Their current role is to make sure that laws are implemented which ensure that landowners get to keep as much as possible of the rent that they collect from their land holdings. This is done by ensuring that land and land rents are taxed as little as possible, and by focusing taxation on employment and trade instead via income tax, national insurance contributions and VAT. This is described in more detail in section 3.1.

Another good example of lawmakers working for the benefit of landowners dates from the discovery of land available for exploitation in the new-found continents of America and Australia. Possession of land there was granted to various British landowners, but the problem was that few people were available to work on it and generate wealth for its owners. The lawmakers came to the landowners' rescue by devising transportation laws for even the most minor offences. The transportees were sent to penal colonies, where they were forced to work as the landowners' slaves.

During the last 100 years, under Labour governments Britain has experienced significant periods when socialist lawmakers were officially in charge. These have not been so amenable to taking on the role of landowners' accomplice. But though the socialists have extracted some concessions from the landowners, they have not been able to dismantle the system of slavery.

2.1.4.2   Law enforcers

The second group of accomplices consists of the top brass of the law enforcers. Their role is to ensure that the property laws devised by the lawmakers are enforced.

The first line of property law enforcers is the increasingly militarised police force. These are supplemented by armies of solicitors, barristers, judges and bailiffs, as well as by the prison system.

If these all fail to quell a rebellion, the last resort of the landowners is the army, which would be called in to enforce the landowners' retention of their land and property. We have seen this happen countless times, both in Britain and in other countries. The British Army swears allegiance to the Crown, the ultimate landowner.

The army, and the armed forces in general, not only protect landowners against internal threats, they also give them protection against external forces. To the slaves, it makes little difference who their landowner is: they are still slaves. To the landowners, it would obviously make a big difference if a new set of external landowners took over the country, because they might lose all control of their land and wealth in the process. There is a famous poster from World War I which shows Lord Kitchener pointing directly at the viewer from a poster captioned 'Your Country Needs You.' More accurate would have been 'Your Owners Need You'.

The heads of the police and the army receive large salaries and lavish perks for what they do, partly to ensure the continued extraction of wealth for the landowners.

2.1.4.3 Company management

It is the responsibility of company managements, the third group of accomplices, to run businesses that generate wealth, and to pass on as much as possible of this wealth to the landowners and as little as possible to the employees, by maximally exploiting the laws and systems created by the lawmakers. They are the equivalent of the overseers and slave drivers in the Caribbean slavery system.

This is a very skilled job, and only people with the highest organisational ability can succeed at it. It is their responsibility to bring together all the resources needed to run a business, including suppliers, machinery, finances, technical skills and customers, and to get them to work together to produce wealth profitably. They also have to be able to ruthlessly implement the system of slavery that the lawmakers have devised.

The landowners do not care what walk of life these managers come from, as long as they deliver the wealth to them. So we hear stories of people from a state school starting off at a low grade in a company and working their way up it and eventually becoming its CEO. Such stories are often cited in the media in order to help create the illusion that we live in a meritocracy where people with particular skills are paid what they are worth. The truth is that if a slave rises to be one of the landowners' major accomplices, they will be vastly overcompensated for their efforts. We know that CEOs are sometimes paid 147 times[13] more than the average wag of their employees. This overcompensation happens all the way down the management chain, the overcompensation reducing in line with the corresponding reduction in responsibility.

2.1.4.4 Bankers

The fourth group of accomplices is comprised of bankers. The Bank of England plays a key role in maintaining the MBSS. It controls the level of unemployment. Just as it is important to maintain a scarcity of land to keep rent high and wages low, it is also important to ensure there is a surplus supply of labour over demand to keep wages low. The book explains this in more detail in section 2.1.7.

Another role of the bankers, especially investment bankers, is to invest the wealth that landowners have obtained and generate further profits from it.

It also seems to be their responsibility to take the blame for the unfair wealth distribution system rather than allowing it to fall fairly on the landowners. For this, they are hugely overcompensated. We have seen how totally corrupt the banks are – there is not a single market that they are not fraudulently manipulating to their advantage. So for many people to lay the blame at the bankers' feet for all the unequal wealth distribution is a natural, but mostly incorrect response, insofar as they are only acting as the landowners' accomplices.

I include in this group of accomplices the roles connected with all financial activities, such as accountants. Accountants are often in league with company management to ensure that as little tax as possible is handed over to the government. They achieve this by fully exploiting the loophole-ridden tax system so that more profit can be handed over to the landowners.

Of course, landowners and accomplices are sometimes one and the same, especially in the case of the bankers.

The Church of England used to be a major accomplice of the landowners, but with the waning of Christian belief their usefulness to the landowners as a tool to control people has lessened. One of Christianity's messages is 'the poor are always with us'. Indeed they are, and they will always be so (and in huge numbers) for as long as they remain enslaved by landowners. I prefer the Christian message of 'do unto others as you would have them do unto you'. So: don't enslave someone else if you wouldn't like them to enslave you.

2.1.5 Landless Slaves

The majority of people in Britain do not own any of the commercial land. The approximately 65% of owner-occupiers who own the land under their own houses are grateful enough to have that. They have little awareness of, or interest in, the existence and ownership of the land where their employer's business is conducted – but it is there that they are enslaved.

To use the board game of Monopoly as an analogy, most of the British population are born into a game of Monopoly where all the sites have already been bought by a couple of players. All the new players can do is to work their way round the board, periodically collecting a minimal £200 for their 'work' and paying rent wherever they land.

Some of the slaves will aspire to rise to becoming accomplices of the landowners. Most of these will be disappointed, because only so many accomplices are required. Most slaves will live out a disappointing, uninspiring life of drudgery at work where they will always feel they are working to make someone else rich. They may look forward to getting home so that they can do something more interesting, creative and rewarding with their spare time and the limited money they receive for their work.

The more wealth the slaves produce, the richer the landowners become, so the slaves are encouraged to work hard, especially by the Conservative Party. Hence their constant refrain of 'hard-working families'. Such statements are the equivalent of the whip wielded on the Caribbean plantations. They are recited in order to stigmatise anyone who is not working hard.

Immigrants are usually landless slaves, and are not objected to by the landowners and their accomplices, who benefit from having cheap personal slaves such as cleaners, gardeners, cooks, drivers, plus cheap workers for their businesses, while at the same time being insulated from the ill effects experienced by those same slaves, such as overcrowding, NHS waiting lists, large class sizes etc. However, the indigenous landless slaves do suffer the ill effects of immigration, which leads to discontent.

2.1.6 Unemployed Slaves

The unemployed are key to the process of extracting wealth from the majority for the benefit of a minority. Their existence is used by the MBSS to help force wages down by ensuring that whenever a vacancy occurs, there will always be someone willing to fill it at even the minimum wage, because that would be slightly better than trying to obtain money from social security, and because already being in work makes it easier to get other work.

It is important that the level of unemployment is maintained at a 'Goldilocks' level – not too high, and not too low. If the level is too high, the unemployed will consume more social security, which means the government may have to raise taxes to pay for it, leading to less wealth for the landowners and a risk of rioting or some other form of civil protest.

If the level of unemployment is too low, there will be too much competition for labour; this will cause wages to rise, reducing company profits. Initially, this may cause businesses to fold, resulting in unemployment and recession. However, a landowner would get nothing if no business was operating on their land, and so their only option is to let their premises at a lower rent, such that companies are able to pay higher wages. So the net effect of rising wages is a reduction in the rent generated for the landowners.

The Bank of England has a euphemism for the situation in which wages are rising above the target inflation rate. They say the economy is 'overheating'. The Bank of England then raises interest rates, which makes more companies fail, thus increasing the level of unemployment back to the 'Goldilocks' level. The Bank of England protects the landowners' extracted wealth at the expense of hundreds of thousands of unemployed people.

The Bank of England call this 'Goldilocks' level 'maximum employment'. In reality, there is no reason for anyone to be unemployed – there's plenty to do. But that wouldn't promote the wealth extraction process.

Despite the MBSS guaranteeing that there will always be unemployment, the unemployed are stigmatised by government in order to encourage them to look for jobs and accept lower wages.

2.1.7   Businesses

Businesses are where the wealth of the country is initially generated and distributed. The money generated from the wealth they produce is then distributed to the interested parties. The book will examine this process of wealth distribution in more detail in section 2.5.

The main distributions of wealth the businesses make after selling the wealth they produce are:
- payments to suppliers – suppliers want to be paid for whatever supplies they have provided to the business,
- wages – to employees,
- taxes – to the government. Corporation tax and business rates are the main ones,
- rent – to the owners of the land and buildings. Businesses normally rent or lease the premises they operate in. Not many have the money needed to buy the freehold of their premises,
- dividends – a share of the profits to the owners of the company,
- interest – usually to banks. Most companies operate with a high level of debt, which they use to buy capital, such as machinery. Interest has to be paid on this debt.

There are six items on the list above. We can see that the last three items on the list are payments to the landowner group. They own the land and premises, they own most of the shares issued by companies, and they own the money which is lent to companies to buy capital. If we assume that payments to suppliers and taxes are fixed, the distribution of wealth becomes a battle between the payments to landholders and the wages paid to workers.

2.1.8 Work

In general, the more we work the more wealth we produce. The amount we work is largely driven by our desires. If we want more wealth we have to work harder. This should be an individual choice, because there are people who do not want much wealth and others who want a great deal of it. Some like a simple life that's not encumbered by a lot of possessions. Some people tilt the work-life balance one way, and others tilt it the other way.

There's no real reason why the government should be involved in influencing people's decisions about whether or not to work hard. It's surely a personal choice. The reason the government, – especially the Conservative government – have used their verbal whips to encourage 'hard-working families' is because they want their slaves to work hard and produce more wealth for the slave owners and their accomplices.

2.1.9 Wealth

In this book, wealth is defined as the product of work being applied to land. Food, clothing, houses, furniture, fuel, cars, electronics, hospitals, schools – the list is endless. Businesses create most of this wealth, and it ultimately comes from humans applying work to land. It makes sense that after a worker has paid their dues to society, they should keep whatever wealth they have created.

In this book money is not considered as wealth. There's not much one can do with it other than use it as a claim on actual wealth (as defined above) or use it to buy the services that help to create wealth.

2.1.10 Capital

Capital is a special subset of wealth. It is not designed to be immediately consumed, but to be used longer-term in the course of wealth production. For example, part of a potato-grower's capital could take the form of a spade. The spade will eventually wear out, and in the meantime it will need to be oiled, cleaned and repaired, but hopefully it will be useful for many seasons of potato-growing.

Capital rightly belongs to the people whose work and skills created it, and they should be able to use it, or sell it, or rent it out as they desire. And if they rent it out, as with a rental car, it ought to be returned at the end of the rental period in the same condition, or else the renter should have to pay for any deterioration.

I cannot think of an economic activity that does not use capital. Businesses can have offices, factories, machinery, computers, vehicles, tools etc. These are all examples of capital that is used in the production of wealth.

In the economic system we have now, which is usually termed *capitalism*, no distinction is made between naturally occurring land and human-made capital. They are both treated as capital that can be owned by individuals or organisations. The alternative system of communism makes the opposite mistake. It rightly allows society to own all the land, but wrongly grants ownership of all privately created capital, such as offices and factories, machinery (the means of production) etc. to society. This results in two mutually antagonistic systems which are both right in one way and wrong in another.

2.1.11 Houses

Houses are capital because they are human-made, but the land underneath them is not. As was explained earlier, landowners create a scarcity of housing land for a growing population, causing the price of housing land to be forced to the maximum that can be afforded, thereby encouraging land speculation.

There are approximately 25 million houses and flats in Britain, and about 65% of them are owner-occupied. The other 35% are rented. However, according to the Leasehold Knowledge Partnership, included in that figure of 65% are 5.37 million leased homes, mostly flats[14]. Leasehold is essentially merely a form of long-term renting. When the lease expires, the home reverts to the owner of the freehold. So in reality, only 43.5% of homes are owner-occupied.

A major factor in the value of the land under a house is its proximity to places of employment and/or transport links. Unfortunately, a factor that now seems to be increasingly dominant is the beauty of its location. Our distorted wealth distribution system means that there are people with so much money that they compete with each other in terms of their ability to pay for second homes in beautiful locations like national parks and the coast – locations that are often far away from lucrative employment. This makes houses in those areas too expensive for the locals who need to work there.

2.2 How wages are forced down

The main goal of the MBSS created by the lawmakers is to allow the wages of employees to be forced down to a minimum, so that the landowners can extract as much wealth as possible from the businesses that created it.

It was explained in section 2.1.2 how rents are forced up to the maximum at the expense of wages. Rents for commercial premises are calculated by the landowner on the assumption that an employer will pay their staff as little as possible (with the caveat that in these partially enlightened days a floor has been established in the form of a legal national minimum wage). Premises are only let when an employer can be found who is prepared to do this. If an enlightened employer wants to pay twice the legal minimum wage for its lowest-skilled jobs, they will not be able to afford the rent.

When a worker responds to a job advertisement, they will be offered a pay rate that corresponds to their skill level and the degree of responsibility entailed in their duties. However, this offer will have been forced to its lowest by the rent payable for the premises. The employer is constrained by the amount of rent they are paying, no matter how much more they might want to pay the prospective employee.

If the worker does not accept the employer's offer there is a pool of other unemployed people maintained by the Bank of England (as was explained in section 2.1.6) who will be willing to accept it. So the worker accepts a wage which is far less than the value of wealth they create.

In sum: the worker is a slave.

Zero-hours contracts, where the employer is not obliged to provide any minimum number of working hours, assist in this process. Using these contracts, a company is able to take on as many workers as it likes without having any financial commitment to them. Company managements are very good at measuring the productivity of their workers. The most productive workers are offered more hours. Less productive workers are offered few or no hours. This turns the workplace into a rat-race and greatly intensifies the effort the slaves must put into their work to achieve the equivalent of even a minimum wage.

The surplus wealth that the slaves produce over and above the cost of their wages is pocketed by the landowners and their accomplices. The book explains the mechanism by which this is achieved in section 2.5.

History has demonstrated how this system, which is based on the ownership of land and the charging of rent for its use, can reduce wages to subsistence levels that force multiple families to live in a single room, working long hours with barely enough to eat. Socialist governments and trade unions have improved this situation, but we are still living in a form of slavery.

A fundamental law of economics is that when all land is owned, wages will be forced down to the minimum that the workers will accept. As productivity rises, slave wages can be kept low, resulting in the landowners and their accomplices becoming richer and richer, as was demonstrated in Thomas Piketty's book *Capital*.

In fact, this law of economics is more a law of human nature. It basically says that people will take as much as they can get. Landowners will push rents up as far as possible at the expense of wages. This is not always the case, but it does seem to be a general pattern in our society.

2.3 Wage Structure

2.3.1 Unskilled or low-skilled workers

The wage structure in the MBSS starts at the bottom with the wages for unskilled and low-skilled work. Unskilled or low-skilled workers are essentially operators of capital. They use tools, tend machines, clean buildings etc. They have skills, but those are normally ones that can be picked up very quickly, such as how to operate a particular machine. Examples are cleaners, shop assistants, construction labourers, machine operators, warehouse workers, packing workers, general labourers etc.

Unskilled labour receives wages that are undercompensated compared to the wealth they assist in producing, as was explained in section 2.2. Wages for unskilled labour are currently propped up by a national legal minimum wage, social security (who wants to work when they can get money for sitting at home doing nothing?), and trade unions – although the power of the unions is much less than it was a few decades ago.

Above the unskilled worker level, differentials in terms of skill and responsibility have to be rewarded, or the system will not work. Few will work harder, take on more responsibility or increase their skills if they are not going to be compensated for it. However, it is the responsibility of company management, under pressure to pay their rent, to squeeze the differentials to ensure that as many employees as possible are undercompensated so that the rent can be paid and profits can be made.

2.3.2   Capital builders and designers

Next up in the pay structure, and analogous to the carpenters working on the Caribbean plantations, are the designers and builders of capital. Examples are architects, builders, engineers, machine designers, computer systems designers, designers of automated equipment and systems, scientific researchers, chemists, biologists etc.

These workers have undergone many years of school, university and workplace training. However, they retain relatively little of the value embedded in what they produce. Instead, this becomes the property of the landowners; the workers receive only their wages.

2.3.3   Entrepreneurs

Next up in the pay structure are successful entrepreneurs. I say 'successful' because the majority of new businesses are actually unsuccessful. Entrepreneurs are people who have a new idea for a business and are prepared to take advantage of the slavery system to get their business running.

2.3.4   Accomplices

Further up in the pay structure are the landowners' accomplices, as defined earlier in the book. The highest paid of these are the CEOs (Chief Executive Officers – the top managers) of large companies. Companies are the source of all the landowners' wealth, and the CEO and his management team have the job of delivering this wealth to the landowners. The CEO delivers it in three forms: Rent for the land and premises used by the company; a share of the company profits in the form of dividends; and interest on the money loaned to the company for the purchase of capital. So the landowners are more than happy to massively overcompensate CEOs for exploiting the workforce, bearing in mind the three huge income streams they generate in return. This overcompensation is reflected all the way down the company's management chains.

The main skills of CEOs are organisational and motivational. It is their responsibility to bring together all the resources needed to run a business, including suppliers, machinery, finances, skills and customers, and to get them to work together to produce wealth profitably. They also have to be able to ruthlessly implement the system of slavery that the lawmakers have devised.

It is common to hear people complaining in the media that CEOs are overpaid. They wonder why the CEO's are not given a pay cut and the money distributed to the shareholders, and why the shareholders don't revolt and insist on lower compensation for CEOs. There seems to be no understanding that the shareholders who own a given company are predominantly landowners, and that they do not mind overcompensating the CEO provided the latter delivers the three huge income streams to the landowner group.

As is explained in the accomplices section 2.1.4.1, lawmakers are essential to the landowners as preservers of their wealth. By 'lawmakers' I primarily mean politicians. But care needs to be taken with the compensation of politicians, because their pay is highly public and they are supposed be representing a lot of people who earn much less than they do. This is circumvented by allowing politicians to earn money by 'consulting', primarily to businesses. Information about this consulting is also available to the public, but it is much less visible than the information about the flat salary they receive. In addition, when a politician's public career is over, they are often rewarded with lucrative jobs with companies.

Bankers – especially investment bankers – are also massively overcompensated for looking after and investing the landowners' money and taking the blame for the inequalities of wealth distribution. They are allowed to keep as bonuses a proportion of the profits they make from the landowners' money.

The top-brass law enforcers in the form of the police and (ultimately) the army are also overcompensated with lavish salaries and perks for ensuring that the landowners will keep their wealth.

2.3.5 Landowners

Whatever surplus remains in a business after the above-mentioned undercompensated wages to slaves and overcompensated wages to accomplices are subtracted is pocketed by the landowners in the form of rent, interest on capital, and a share of the company profits.

In summary, the wage structure described above is clearly a meritocracy to the extent that the harder someone works and the more they improve their skills, the more they will be compensated, especially when they become a significant accomplice of the landowners. However, it is a meritocracy that is embedded within a hidden system of slavery which few can see. The parallel with the Caribbean slavery system is clear.

2.3.6   Public sector

Wages in the public sector largely reflect those in the private sector. Managers in the public sector receive similarly high wages for their skill at suppressing the wages of their slaves.

2.4 Formation of capital

A further point about landowners is that they not only own the land, but most of everything else that is worth owning – capital. This was shown in the HMRC figures in section 1.1. The landowners receive the rent from land, and they are able to lend that money out at interest to the government, to businesses and to people who want a mortgage.

In order to create capital, society must forgo some consumption and invest instead in capital. Section 1.3.3 presents the example of a plantation owner who, rather than spending his money on more luxury goods, instead chose to pay the wages of a slave (food, clothing, shelter) in order to build additional capital, such as a building.

Slavery is like an enforced savings system in which the slaves are forced through low wages to forgo consumption so that capital can be created. The problem with this is that all the capital ends up in the hands of the landowners, and it is only the slaves who have to forgo their consumption. The land-owning minority can consume luxury goods to their hearts' content and still have plenty to invest in capital that will make them even wealthier.

Landowners take ownership of most companies. We see examples of this process in microcosm on the TV programme *Dragon's Den,* where a panel of rich entrepreneurs sit like vultures while new entrepreneurs, starved of investment capital, present their start-up businesses in the hope of getting money to buy capital. In order to obtain this capital the new entrepreneurs must sacrifice a large portion of the ownership of their fledgling businesses to the rich entrepreneurs. The resultant emotional turmoil passes for entertainment.

It is a common myth that the majority of shares in companies are bought and held by pension funds from which the majority benefit. According to ONS statistics, the reality is that UK pension funds and insurance companies (of which mostly the rich benefit) hold about 9%[15]. The 'rest of the world' owns 54%, which is a large figure but there are many foreign companies, some of them very large, listed on the London stock exchange. Individuals own 9%. Most of the remainder is in private hands one way or another. For example, 'other financial institutions' hold 7.1%. These will be predominantly shares owned by investment banks on behalf of their private clients, using a mechanism called nominee accounts. The way that nominee accounts work is as follows: private clients give their money to an investment bank who then create a nominee account for each client. The bank pools this money and uses it to buy large numbers of shares in its own name which it then allocates internally *pro rata* to the private clients' nominee accounts. For an annual fee, the investment bank undertakes all the management of their private clients' shares in the nominee accounts, including the collection of dividends. To the outside world it appears as if the shares are owned by an institutional investment bank, whereas in reality they are held by the investment bank on behalf of an individual or organisation.

Another common myth is that much of the commercial land is owned by pension funds. As we can see from the earlier table of the top 10 landowners, pension funds hold less than 1% of the land.

So as a group, landowners own not only most of the land, but also most of our companies and most of the debt. From these three sets of assets they collect rent, dividends and interest respectively.

2.5 Wealth production and distribution

In previous sections I described the mechanism by which wages are forced as low as possible, and the wage structure that results. In this section I will go into more detail concerning the mechanisms by which wealth is distributed.

2.5.1 Initial distribution of wealth

The initial distribution of wealth occurs in businesses, where most of Britain's wealth is created.

The main purpose of a business is to produce wealth or to assist other businesses in the production of wealth. Let us imagine a growing business and walk through how it is structured to see how wealth is distributed by the business.

Suppose two entrepreneurs create a business to manufacture an interesting new gadget. At first they design the gadget in their own time, in their garage, at their own expense.

If they think the gadget will sell they may plan a small trial production run of the gadget. This requires more money. If they already have the money themselves they can cover the cost. This is where landowners are at an advantage, because they can start up a business cheaply using the money they have previously taken from the wealth produced by slaves. If the entrepreneurs do not have the necessary money, they may be able to borrow it from a bank if they can make a satisfactory business case.

Suppose that they do not have the money, but have been able to persuade their bank to give them a loan. The loan will have come predominantly from landowner money deposited at the bank, because the majority of wealth is owned by a small minority. The entrepreneurs will have to pay interest on that loan. This interest represents the first and continuing extraction of wealth the landowners will make from the business.

Suppose that the trial production run goes well, and the gadgets are bought enthusiastically at the local car boot sale. The entrepreneurs now plan to go into production in a bigger way. They rent a small factory premises from landowners. The rent is set, on the advice of the landowner's agents, at a level which the market can bear, which is always based on the assumption that the wages of the factory workers will be set as low as possible. If enlightened entrepreneurs come along who want to pay their employees more, the business will likely fail because they will not be able to afford the rent.

Note that the entrepreneurs only rent the premises. There is no possibility of the business buying the freehold of their premises, which would require a much larger loan. This is true of the majority of businesses. The premises they operate from are predominantly owned by the landowners to whom they pay rent.

The landowner group are now receiving two streams of revenue: the interest on the loan, and the rent for the premises.

The entrepreneurs also buy some machines to manufacture their gadget and some raw materials with which to make their gadgets, and they recruit additional employees. This all requires more money, and they raise it in two ways. The first is via additional loans from the bank, which has been persuaded with the help of a new business plan. The second is from selling some of the ownership of the company. This process can be seen on the previously-mentioned TV show *Dragon's Den* where rich individuals (usually not landowners, but entrepreneurs who have become rich as company managers) give money to a start-up business in return for a large share of the ownership of the company and therefore a large share of the potential future profits of the company. *Dragon's Den* tends to feature small start-up businesses. Most small businesses will borrow from a bank. For larger businesses, there exist venture capital funds in which landowners have invested their money to be lent to companies, or to take ownership of them.

As a business grows, it may access extra funding by conducting an IPO (initial public offering). In an IPO, additional shares in the business are sold to 'the public'. In reality, the shares are predominantly sold to the euphemistically-termed 'institutions', which are mistakenly understood by most people to be pension funds and insurance companies, but which are in reality primarily investment banks that are buying them on behalf of rich clients who hold nominee accounts with them.

When there is a large government privatisation IPO, like the recent Post Office IPOs (2013 and 2015), a large portion of the shares are reserved for 'institutions', and many of these end up in the nominee accounts of the institutions' private clients. This is a huge scam for benefiting the landowners. The media's economic reporters will state in the news that the shares were mostly bought by institutions, and nobody will question it.

The landowner group is now receiving three streams of income from the business: interest on loans, rent for land, and a share of the profits in the form of dividends. Meanwhile, the employees' share of the wealth produced by the new company is always forced to a minimum, as was described in earlier sections. The slaves do not see these three streams of income, which disappear long before they get anywhere near their wage packets, so they have no idea how much of the wealth they have produced is being stolen from them by the landowners.

Initially, the management of the company is unable to take much in the way of a salary from their business. They have to work extremely hard to get their business through its early years. But as the business grows and produces more wealth for the landowners, the latter, who have become the major shareholders, allow the company management – their accomplices – to be vastly overcompensated.

It interesting to note that although the Conservative Party always claim to be pro-business, they are actually the deadly enemy of business. The landowner group they represent are continually extracting wealth from businesses in the form of rent, dividends and interest. The result is that businesses are continually starved of the ability to invest in capital using the wealth they have produced. To buy capital to expand they must borrow yet more money from the landowner group in the form of corporate debt or a new issuance of shares. This of course results in even more interest or dividends being paid to the landowner group.

2.5.2   Secondary redistribution of wealth

The secondary redistribution of wealth is performed by the government.

The first intervention by the government is achieved through taxation. Governments use taxes to fund communal needs like road building, the justice system, defence, welfare etc.; but the other role of taxation is to redistribute wealth in order to compensate for the fact that the primary distribution of wealth performed in businesses that was described in section 2.5.1 is so unsatisfactory.

Over the years, governments have designed a tax system that aims to take from the landowners and their accomplices (the rich pay most of the tax) some of the wealth they have stolen from the slaves, and hand it back to the slaves. The book will describe this complex, unfair, inefficient, expensive, loophole-ridden tax system in greater detail in section 3.1.

The major forms in which wealth is redistributed back to the slaves are:

- free health service via such forms of wealth as hospitals, medicines, trained doctors, nurses and surgeries. This is available to all, although the rich have so much money that they can afford to use private healthcare instead,

- free education for children via such forms of wealth as schools, books, playing fields and trained teachers. This is also available to all, although here too the rich have so much money that they can afford to use private schools instead,
- state pensions. These are also available to all, even though the rich normally also have private pensions that have benefited from generous tax rebates from the government,
- housing benefit (which is then often handed over to private landlords to pay their inflated rents)
- welfare payments.

The second intervention by the government takes the form of borrowing. The landowners and their accomplices acquire a lot of wealth that has been stolen from the slaves – so much so that they cannot consume it all. This is especially the case now, because taxes on the rich have been reduced. The highest rate of income tax fifty years ago was 98%, whereas it is now only 45%. The government borrows money from the landowners by issuing them with interest-bearing government bonds. The government then uses this money to distribute wealth to the slaves in the form of health care, education, tax credits, welfare payments and pensions. The government gets into debt, and the debt rises year after year, as do the interest payments on that debt. The book will talk more about government debt in section 3.5.

Not all secondary wealth distribution goes to the slaves. A large portion of it actually goes back to the landowners and their accomplices.

DEFRA (the Department for Environment, Food and Rural Affairs) pays over £2bn per year in grants to landowning farmers[16]. The EU's Common Agricultural Policy pays out nearly £1bn per year to UK farmers[17].

People contributing to their private pensions receive tax relief at their marginal rate on the contributions, which is added to their pension fund. However. it is mostly the rich and middle classes who pay significant amounts into private pension funds. In 2014-15 this cost the government £34.2 billion in tax relief[18], not including the national insurance relief on employer contributions. Note that this relief alone is bigger than the entire 2013-14 tax credits budget of £30 billion paid to the less well-off[19].

In addition, the Conservatives have introduced pension drawdown, which allows the rich (because they are the ones who make significant contributions to private pensions) to take 25% of their private pension pot tax-free, rather than having it all converted to an annuity and paying income tax on income from that annuity.

The arts of the rich are funded by the theatre tax relief which gives reductions on the income earned by theatres. Additionally, professional production houses such as the Royal Opera House, Royal Albert Hall, National Theatre, Southbank Centre and Globe theatre have been granted charitable status, which means that they can claim 25% tax on all contributions received.

The rich are the main users of ISAs. The estimated Exchequer cost of the tax relief for ISAs in 2015-16 was around £2.6 billion[20].

2.5.3   Changes to the secondary redistribution of wealth

It is always interesting to watch the economic analysts' reaction to changes in the tax system when the Chancellor of the Exchequer announces the government's annual budget, because the analysts treat the changes as static. That is, when a taxation change is made that will change the distribution of wealth, the analysts assume that the change will be permanent, or at least that it will stay until a further tax change is made. The analysts apparently do not realise that the MBSS is a dynamic system controlled by economic laws, and that the primary law is that wages are always forced to the lowest level that the workers will accept.

So when the Chancellor announces a 5p cut in the basic rate of income tax, the media's economics analysts all declare that this will be good for workers, because they will get to keep that extra money in their wage packets. What is not recognised is that the slavery system is a dynamic system, with its own laws that work to counter any changes that are made in order to benefit the slaves.

As soon as the change is implemented, the workers are 5p in the pound better off than previously, i.e. they are earning 5p in the pound more than they would previously accept. The primary rule of economics will immediately start working on this. Businesses cannot simply cut wages across the board to absorb the 5p benefit the slaves have received, but the next time a retailer rents a shop, for example, the rent required by the landowner will be increased to absorb that 5p in the pound, and the retailer will be forced to offer any newly hired staff 5p in the pound less (subject to the constraints imposed by the legal minimum wage). Tax cuts always end up in the pockets of the landowners – which is why the Conservative government always preaches a low-tax environment.

2.5.4   Net result of the wealth redistribution

After the enormously complex, loophole-ridden, time-wasting, costly process of the secondary redistribution of wealth, we are still left with an unfair distribution, as follows:

- landowners are receiving an inflated rent for land they have no right to own. Even if they pay back 45% of this in income tax, they are still getting 55% of rent that doesn't belong to them,
- landowners are extracting more wealth from their slaves than is handed back to the slaves via the tax system,
- accomplices are overcompensated for assisting the landowners,
- workers are caught between two pincer jaws: their wages are forced as low as possible, and the rent for their housing (or the price they pay for their housing) is forced to a maximum,
- millions of demoralized, demotivated people are on minimum wages and low wages which in no way reflect their true worth, and where the benefits they receive from a secondary redistribution of wealth are always under the threat of removal by a Conservative government that is interested mostly in increasing the wealth of the landowning minority.

2.6 Landowners' strategies for maintaining their wealth

The landowners want to acquire as much wealth as possible, but they realise that if they take too much they risk precipitating a revolution and losing everything they currently have. So over the years, as the production of wealth has increased, they have had to implement a variety of strategies in order to maintain and increase their wealth.

2.6.1 Anonymity

It's very difficult to attack a system if the main beneficiaries of that system are anonymous. The poor old Duke of Westminster is always the first to be blamed because he appears on all the rich lists. People might also know about other large estates in London such as the Cadogan and de Walden estates. However, the rest of the landowners are fairly anonymous, and they much prefer it that way. Some of the strategies used to preserve their anonymity are:

- they make it very difficult to discover who owns all the land – only 84% of it is currently registered[21]. It costs £3 to find out from the Land Registry who owns a given property, so it would cost many millions of pounds and several lifetimes of work to perform an analysis of UK land ownership,
- they don't voluntarily register land with the Land Registry,
- they hide their ownership of land in trusts if necessary,
- they conduct land rental agreements through land agents or estate agents in order to remain as anonymous as possible. It takes a very hard-

hearted person to be able to take rent from people who are unable to afford it, and to increase that rent each year. Using an agent to carry out this work removes the direct contact and the guilt that goes with it, and the agent can salve their own conscience by claiming they are merely carrying out the landowner's instructions,

- they socialise mainly with fellow landowners and senior accomplices, for instance by going to the exclusive, expensive enclosures at Henley Royal Regatta and Ascot, Wimbledon, their exclusive "gentlemen's clubs" in London, the opera, or hunts and shoots. (Read George Monbiot's article on how the Conservative government subsidises the sporting pastimes of the rich) [22],
- they send their children to private schools with fellow landowners' children – preferably to Eton
- they don't participate in any surveys of wealth,
- they keep out of the media, and refrain from public or ostentatious displays of wealth.

2.6.2 Spreading confusion

The landowners' second strategy is to spread confusion. The more fuzzy the system appears to be, the less other people can successfully contest it. The ways they confuse others and distract them from perceiving the truth are as follows:

The landowners pretend, via the Conservative Party's propaganda, that we live in a pure meritocracy where everyone gets what they deserve – no more, no less – and those who don't do well should be despised. It's amazing how many people believe this message. Unfortunately, since the MBSS is so confusing, and since the media present so many examples of people rising to become well-paid accomplices, it is relatively easy to persuade people that they live in a pure meritocracy. It's only by observing the basic principles at work – i.e. how the commercial land is owned by a minority who use their control to force down wages – that it is possible to see through the charade of this supposed pure meritocracy.

The landowners make the system as complex as possible, so that nobody understands what the causes and effects are. Instead of being able to see the big picture, everybody gets bogged down in minor details. We see a lot of people protesting about the current situation of wealth inequality, such as the Occupy groups. Some will put the blame on the bankers, some will blame corporations, others 'capitalism', the money system, the tax system, globalism, the establishment, the EU, immigration, the Illuminati, the fact that we've left the gold standard – the list is endless. But when they are asked what the solution is, they don't know. They know something is wrong, but they don't know how to fix it.

The landowners like to present themselves as meritocrats. TV shows that feature some of them doing up their estate's tea shop help to create the illusion of an impoverished aristocracy that is struggling just to get by. While one or two of them may be in this position, most are not.

The landowners and their accomplices like to present themselves as benefactors to society by noisily giving back to charity a little of what they have quietly stolen from the slaves. Attending lavish charity balls is one such strategy.

Another astute move by the Conservative Party was to allow more people to own their own little snippet of land – the land under their homes – by selling off the state-owned council houses to their occupiers at discounted prices. As I explained earlier, most people are simply blind to the ownership of commercial land, so whenever anybody talks about land issues their attention immediately turns to the only patch of land they have and know about – namely, that which is sitting under their own homes – and they become terrified that somebody is going to take it from them. If these people realised that in acreage terms housing land only accounts for about 5% of the total, and that they are really entitled to a share of the rent from the other 95% of the land, they might be less terrified.

2.6.3   Concessions

If the above strategies fail, the landowners have to make some concessions by agreeing to hand over some of their wealth to the slaves, especially if the alternative is a revolution. These concessions have normally been achieved under pressure from socialist governments.

The biggest concessions have been state education, the National Health Service, and state pensions. The wages of the majority of slaves are not high enough to pay for the education of their children, or to pay doctors and dentists for tending to the needs of their families. So a concession was made whereby the landowners would pay for these services in the form of increased taxes. The landowners still extract wealth from the slaves, but the tax system takes some of it back and uses it to pay for state-provided education, health and pensions.

Fortunately for the rich, they benefit much more from state pensions than do the poor. According to the Office for National Statistics, from 2012 to 2014 the life expectancy for newborn baby boys was highest in Kensington and Chelsea (83.3 years) and lowest in Blackpool (74.7 years) – nearly nine years' difference[23].

2.6.4   Landowner strategies in recessions

In recessions, the landowners fight to keep hold of as much wealth as possible by keeping their rents high. The last thing landowners want is to see their rents reduced. So at the first sign of a recession, the landowners start complaining in the media (via their accomplices) that the business rates for the businesses renting their land are too high, even though these rates are only of the order of 25% of the rents they are charging their tenants.

The landowners will also ask councils to reduce their car parking fees to encourage customers to shop at their businesses. In effect, this represents a transfer of wealth from local government to themselves to enable them to keep their rents high.

The landowners will also ask councils to invest more in the vicinity of commercial land such as shopping centres, in order to attract greater footfall. This too is a transfer of wealth that is intended to keep rents high.

2.6.5   Acquisition of more land, bonds and shares

When the landowners are undertaxed, as now, they accumulate claims on wealth (money) and are unable to spend it fast enough. They pass some of their excess money to their investment bank, which invests it on their behalf in more land, shares and bonds. From these assets the landowners collect rent, dividends and interest, becoming even wealthier. More and more British assets are falling into the hands of the landowning minority. The majority of the population is becoming poorer and poorer, with the middle classes gradually disappearing.

2.7 Traditional economic analysis

A traditional economic analysis identifies three primary factors in the production of wealth: land, capital and work. Some economists claim that entrepreneurs deserve to be treated as a fourth primary factor because of their energy and generation of ideas, but here I am including entrepreneurs under the work factor.

Subsequent to such an analysis, it is natural to say that the wealth produced should be given to the owners of the three factors in proportion to the relative strength of their claims: land via rent and subject to the quality of the land; capital via interest and subject to the rate of interest; and work via wages and subject to the merit of the work.

However, there is a fourth claim on the wealth produced, one that Margaret Thatcher said does not exist, and that is society. A civilized society has a claim on the wealth produced in order to look after those in society who are unable to look after themselves, and in order to build and maintain social capital such as roads, educated and trained people, justice systems, the health service etc. Society makes its claim on produced wealth via taxes, and is subject to the rate of taxation.

If we examine the three traditional factors of production we can plainly see that societal capital underpins each one of them. It is society that helps increase the rent of land by building societal capital around sites, and it is society that helps improve the merit of work by educating and training people. So it is evident that a civilized society has a just claim on any wealth produced.

The book has shown that when land is privately owned, it has the power to take more than its fair share of wealth at the expense of the claims of work and society, which is the cause of slavery.

In any economic downturn the landowners, via their political wing, i.e. the Conservative Party, will seek to protect their claims to wealth at the expense of society's claim, by reducing the funding for society's services.

2 The Operation of the Modern British Slavery System

3 The Impact of the MBSS

This section describes how the MBSS described in section 2 affects most aspects of our lives.

3.1 Tax system

This section is quite detailed in some areas. For anybody who wants to skip it, its main points are that the current tax system is:

- unfair, in that it fails to tax the true value of land that society has created,
- inefficient, in that it fails to collect taxes such as corporation tax from global companies,
- full of loopholes that armies of accountants seek to exploit,
- expensive to administer, because it is so complex.

Rather than charging rent on land as a means of raising income for communal projects, the lawmakers have devised a freehold system whereby landowners do not have to pay society any rent for their land. This means that landowners are able to set aside huge areas of land for their own leisure purposes, such as for shooting, hunting and fishing, but never have to pay anything to society for this privilege.

It also means that landowners can collect rent from tenants who make use of the landowner's land. Even if the landlord pays tax on this income, they are still getting a stream of revenue for something that doesn't rightfully belong to them.

This is bad enough in relation to unimproved land like farmland, but it is appalling when it comes to land that has been massively improved by society, such as the land located in the heart of our towns and cities. The value of the land at the heart of any city has grown massively as society has invested in it in the form of roads, water and sewage systems, electricity and gas networks, rail, bus stations, railway stations, underground trains, high-speed trains, airports, civic buildings, royal palaces, national museums and art galleries, national theatres, national sports arenas, parks, police forces, fire brigades etc. The landowners are taking a good proportion of all the value of societally-created improvements in the form of rent.

The consequences of not collecting land rent is that we have instead the current massively complex tax system which is expensive to administer and is full of loopholes that accountants are able to exploit. MPs, the House of Lords and a vast number of civil servants waste the majority of their time debating and implementing these tax systems and their associated exceptions and allowances. HMRC has an annual budget of £3.58 bn (2015-15) [24] for collecting the current taxes; meanwhile, landowners, companies and their accomplices employ armies of accountants to avoid paying tax to HMRC.

Some of the wealth stolen from the slaves by the landowners is taken back by the government via the tax system and redistributed by various government agencies to the undercompensated in the form of the National Health Service, education, tax credits, Job Seekers' Allowance, housing benefits, etc. What a waste of time and effort, most of which would be eliminated by simply collecting the full value of the rent of land for society!

3.1.1 Single tax?

If we were to ask an employee of a business whether they had ever paid income tax, they would likely reply in the affirmative. Likewise for other taxes: VAT, National Insurance, Council Tax etc. If we then asked the employee where they'd got the money to pay all those taxes, they would reply that it came in their pay. So in fact, employees do not pay tax: their employer pays it, and the employee is merely a conduit to the exchequer. The employee feels as if they are paying the tax because if income tax is reduced by the government, the employee temporarily has more money. Admittedly, the amount of VAT paid by an employee depends to some extent on what they spend their pay on, because there is no VAT on food and children's clothing (for example), but on average, as a percentage of income it is fairly predictable.

To establish how much tax a business is actually paying, we need to add up the taxes that the business itself pays, such as business rates and corporation tax, plus all the taxes that it puts into its employees' pay.

Wouldn't it be a lot simpler for everyone if the business made a single tax payment direct to the exchequer, and then whatever the employees received in their wage packet could then be spent without having to pay any form of additional tax? It's so confusing at the moment to be told how much a job pays, and then have to work out by deducting tax just how much of that pay remains. If someone gets a £1000 rise it doesn't mean that they will be £1000 better off, because half of it may be taken in income tax and National Insurance deductions. What an inefficient system – and it's all been invented merely in order to allow landowners not to pay land rent!

63

3.1.2 Income tax

Income tax is a very arbitrary tax because it takes little account of the value of land. Take as an example a very simple business like busking. Suppose the busker pays no rent for his pitch and his only other expenses are for an occasional guitar string – in other words, they are negligible. Let us suppose that the busker occupies a pitch which allows him to play all year round. His pitch is in a prime location in the town centre, so it has enough passers-by to generate a total of £30,000 in contributions over the year. The busker is honest when filling in his tax return, and after a tax-free allowance of £10,000 he pays 20% tax (i.e. £4,000) on the remaining £20,000, which means that he takes home £26,000, assuming no other taxes.

The next year the same busker, who continues to apply the same skills and same amount of effort in his work, is assigned a different, marginal pitch with less footfall that is slightly away from the centre of town, so that he attracts only £15,000 in contributions from passers-by. After a £10,000 tax-free allowance the busker pays 20% tax on the remaining £5,000, which works out at £1,000, meaning he busker takes home £14,000, assuming no other taxes.

So the result is that the same busker, applying the same amount of skill and effort, takes home £26,000 in one year and £14,000 in the next. The income tax system has completely failed to reflect the full value of the prime pitch which the busker used for the first year. The lesson it conveys is that if you work on more valuable land, the income tax rules will let you keep more of the value that was created by society rather than that which you created through your own work.

A similar analysis could be applied to shops. Due to the way the income tax system works, shops in a prime location keep more of the value created by society, although the difference is simply pocketed by the landowner in the form of much higher rents and profits. This explains why shops at the margins of towns and cities are significantly more likely to go bust in the event of a recession, and why the occupants of these marginal sites change more often than shops in prime locations.

Income tax tries to compensate for its arbitrariness by being progressive. The more someone earns, the higher the percentage of tax they pay on that extra income. Of course the Conservative Party fights against this, whereas socialists support it. Since the 1970s, when the top rate of income tax was as high as 98%, the lawmaker accomplices have gradually reduced the highest rates of income tax. It is no coincidence that the rich have become correspondingly much richer. The landowners and their accomplices now have so much money that they don't know what to do with it except buy more land, shares and bonds.

It is worth noting that although income tax is accepted as a fundamental part of our 'capitalist' system, it is effectively a communist idea. The harder someone works, and the more they improve their skills, the more they earn in the slave meritocracy, and so the more income tax they pay. That effectively implies that at least some of the value generated by a person's hard work and skills belongs to society – a notion that approaches a very communist ideal.

Under the current tax regime, socialists who seek to take the unearned wealth pocketed by landowners can only do so by increasing tax rates. But this would also penalise those who are genuinely working hard to produce wealth, with the risk that they might take their skills and hard work elsewhere. This gives the landowners and their accomplices a powerful argument for not raising income tax rates.

National Insurance contributions are a tax which works in a similar way to income tax, but with different thresholds and different rates, and with employers also making a contribution. I won't treat it separately here; I'll merely note that it represents just another complication in an already over-complex system.

In sum: both income tax and National Insurance contributions are taxes on employment. The higher the tax, the more the employer has to pay.

3.1.3 Value-added tax

Value-Added Tax (VAT) is a tax on trading. Whenever something is bought, other than for a few exceptions such as food and children's clothing, which have been created to mitigate the impact of the tax on the poorest in society, a current rate of 20% tax is levied on the buyer by the seller, who passes the tax collected on to the Exchequer.

We often hear free trade with other countries being advocated; but the 20% VAT levied on most transactions means we don't even have free trade in our high streets.

VAT is another form of tax which fails to capture the value of land. Like income tax, it takes a much bigger proportion of the income earned on sites located on marginal land than that earned on sites located on prime land, and thus causes unemployment.

VAT can be avoided with cash transactions that lack paper or computer records of the trade. Well-known examples of this are such tradesmen's services as plumbers and builders. Thus VAT tempts us all to be criminal tax evaders.

In summary: VAT is a drag on trade, because it adds a burden of administration and forces sellers to be unpaid tax collectors for the Exchequer. It is unfair, because it does not take account of the value of the land held by society. It hits the poorest hardest, and it tempts people to become criminals.

However, VAT serves the landowners well because it is not a tax on land, and it adds another element of complexity to the tax system that helps to bamboozle most people about the fairness of the current system we live in.

3.1.4   Corporation tax

Corporation tax is a rather complex tax on company profits. It has recently proved to be uncollectable from global corporations, because they are able to shift their profits to parts of the world that have either no or low corporation tax. If instead the full value of rent for land was collected, these problems would not occur.

One of the global companies involved in the corporation tax controversy was Google (now renamed Alphabet). In these days of business being conducted over the internet, it is interesting to consider where the full value of rent for land should fall. For example, in 2000 the Labour government auctioned off the next generation of mobile phone licences. Telecom companies were bidding simply for the right to use the bandwidth necessary for transmitting their signals over the airwaves.

Through this auction the government raised an unexpectedly large £22.5 bn to cover the rent for twenty years' use of these airwave bandwidths[25]. Since the airwaves are included in the definition of land set out in section 2.1.1, the government was effectively collecting a land rent. Google's traffic over electronic networks would need to be similarly considered in a true assessment of the land rent that is owed to society.

3.1.5   Inheritance tax

Inheritance tax mostly taxes the value of inherited land, although there are many complex loopholes and exceptions which impede the collection of this tax.

The value of housing land has risen so much recently that more people are being caught by inheritance tax, although the percentage of estates that attract inheritance tax is still very low. If society were to take the full value of land rent, inheritance tax would not be required because land would not be worth anything to an individual; it would only be worth something to the true owner – society.

At the end of their life, people should be free to pass on whatever they have accumulated to whomever they please, as long as they have paid a fair rent for the land they prevented society from using during the accumulation process.

It's not really worth taxing inherited human-made wealth because most of it just decays over time, and money has to be spent by the inheritor to maintain it.

3.1.6   Council Tax

Council Tax is a tax on houses and flats. It replaced the Community Charge (nicknamed the Poll Tax) which was brought in in the late 1980s. The Community Charge had to be quickly withdrawn, because it was so regressive that it provoked numerous riots.

The council tax is capped, and bears little relation to the value of the land that the occupants of a given house are depriving society of, especially in the case of more expensive properties. The fallacious argument used to justify this lack of relationship to land value is that council tax pays only for services such as refuse collection and the fire service, so everybody benefits and everyone should therefore pay a similar amount.

3.1.7   Business rates

Business rates are a sort of rent that society collects from a business for the value of the location that a business occupies. This tax is quite small in relation to the value of the commercial land being occupied.

3.1.8   Capital Gains Tax

CGT is a complicated tax that was introduced by a socialist government in 1965 with the purpose of taxing speculators in assets such as land and companies.

It is mainly applies only to the landowners and their accomplices because they are the ones who own most of the assets. Hence it is a tax that the Conservative party are constantly trying to reduce and which the socialists are trying to increase.

3.1.9 Sin taxes

A sin tax is an excise tax specifically levied on certain goods or activities that are deemed potentially harmful to society, such as alcohol, tobacco, sugary drinks and gambling. Sin taxes are used to increase the price of these goods in an effort to reduce their use.

Perhaps another reason for sin taxes is to prevent the performance of the slave workforce from being impaired, because this would be undesirable from the landowners' perspective. Recreational drugs such as hallucinogens, opiates and amphetamines are made illegal rather than taxed.

3.2 Politics

Since we live in a slave society, it is natural that politics largely divides us into two groups: the landowners and their accomplices, who want to keep as much as possible of the wealth that their slaves produce; and the slaves, who also want to keep as much as possible of the wealth they produce. The metaphor commonly used for this division is the 'right' and the 'left'.

The representatives of the right and the left sit in the House of Commons and spend most of their time arguing over the distribution of wealth, with no sign that any of them actually understand the slavery system that distributes the wealth.

3.2.1 The Conservative Party

The Conservative Party (which is politically on 'the right') represents the landowners and their accomplices. It was formed in 1830s, when Robert Peel reformed the Tory party. The objective of his new party was to 'conserve the monarchy and the peerage' – in other words, to benefit the landowners. Since then, with inceasing enfranchisement of the vote the party has had to necessarily put a peg on its nose and expand its reach downwards to the class of lesser landowners. The main objective of the Conservative Party is to preserve the MBSS.

The party is funded by landowners and their major accomplices, such as CEOs of large companies and hedge fund managers, who often make donations of their stolen wealth in order to obtain a peerage. Through these donations they are clearly able to influence the policies of the Conservative Party.

It might seem puzzling that in a supposed democracy such a small group of landowners is able to remain in power. How is it possible for a minority of landowners to prevail against a majority of slaves? However, it must be realised that among the supporters of the landowners are the landowners' accomplices who, as was explained earlier, are hugely overcompensated for their assistance. There are also the aspiring accomplices who hope one day to become managers, politicians, policemen etc. Then there are the people who see only the system of meritocracy embedded in the slavery system, and who believe that the Conservative Party is made up of the best people for operating this system. Finally, there are those who are simply scared by the Conservative Party's rhetoric into believing that a system different from the current one would be unworkable. Many people are confused and don't understand that the Conservatives represent the slave owners – especially when the Conservative party continually describes Britain as 'one nation' and claims that "We're all in it together".

The Conservative Party unfortunately provides a natural home for those who are happy to prey on the other members of society. In other words: those who are looking to make a profit from the work of others; those who are looking for self-enrichment at the expense of others; and those who are not willing to share the world's resources fairly with others.

The Conservatives won the 2015 election with only 24.3% of the possible votes[26]. If the people who are doing very nicely out of the slavery system can be relied on to vote, then less than a quarter of the eligible voters are needed to win an election. The beneficiaries of the MBSS system are highly motivated to vote. They have a lot to lose, and so they turn out in force at the polls. The slaves, on the other hand, are generally demotivated and confused by the system, and so tend to not to vote.

The mantra of the Conservative Party is 'work hard'. They constantly refer to 'hard-working families'. They want their slaves to work hard, because the harder they work, the richer the landowners become. But is it really any business of the government whether people work hard or not? Surely that is an individual's choice.

Another mantra of the Conservative Party is 'low taxes'. There's a reason for this. Taxes are predominantly paid by the rich, and are distributed by the government to the less well-off in the form of a state-provided health service, state education for the children of the slaves, tax credits etc. Given the fundamental economic law whereby wages are always forced to a minimum, changes in taxation have no long-term effect on wages, so the less tax is taken from the slave owners, the wealthier they become.

They also try to convince everyone that they live in a meritocracy in which everyone gets what they deserve. Anyone who does well for themselves by becoming one of the well-paid accomplices is also keen to promote this idea.

The Conservative Party does recognise that there is poverty in Britain, but their solution to poverty is always 'education', with no recognition that the MBSS is designed to force the wages of workers as low as possible irrespective of a person's education. We see this currently, with many graduates having to take minimum-wage jobs when they leave university.

To confuse people more, the Conservative Party has recently announced an increase in the minimum wage for those aged 25 years and over. This could be seen as merely a political gimmick to solve a political problem, namely the embarrassingly large degree of youth unemployment. Employers are clearly going to opt to employ people under 25 to perform low-wage jobs, because the legal minimum wage is only two thirds of the minimum wage for those over 25. Youth unemployment will be decreased at the expense of increased adult unemployment.

3.2.2   The Labour Party

The Labour Party generally represents the slaves – those who own little and have only their labour to sell. It is funded mostly by trade unions who raise money from the slaves they represent.

The main strategy of the Labour Party is to accept the mechanics of the MBSS described in this book, but to mitigate it through two policies designed to produce a fairer distribution of wealth. The first of these two policies is to take wealth from the landowners and their accomplices by raising their taxes, and then distribute this wealth to the slaves in the form of healthcare, education, tax credits and pensions. The second is to increase the wages of the slaves by setting a legal national minimum wage.

The Labour Party's roots are in international socialism, which believes in the free movement of people. However, in these days of high UK immigration, this gives the Labour Party a big problem. Immigrants tend to arrive in the UK owning nothing, and so they are slaves and compete for the jobs of the UK's indigenous slaves, forcing down wages and working conditions. The Labour Party's failure to decisively combat immigration, which it had very little power to do in any case, because of the EU´s rules guaranteeing the free movement of labour between its member states, alienates the indigenous slaves from the Labour Party.

3.2.3   The Liberal Democrats

The Liberal Democrats (formerly known as the Liberal Party) have lost their way, and it is difficult to see what exactly they stand for at the moment. They seem to occupy territory somewhere between the Labour and Conservative parties, and they consequently attract few votes. However, a hundred years ago the Liberals believed that people should pay rent to society for any land they occupied, and that there should be no other taxes. The revenue from this rent would be used for communal purposes such as road building, justice and defence, and for looking after those who were too old, too young, too sick or too disabled to look after themselves.

The benefit of such a system is that it would completely dismantle the slavery system we currently have, because the minority would no longer have control over land, hence no control over people. If someone wanted to use land, they should pay society a rent for it. This means that land would always be available to anyone willing to pay the rent. Landowners would no longer control the level of wages, because if a worker did not wish to accept an employer's wage offer they could simply rent a piece of land from society at the margin, where the rent is zero, and set up and operate their own business.

3.2.4   The Communist Party

Communists seek a fairer distribution of wealth and an end to the slavery system. They believe that land should not be private property. This is entirely justified in my view, as I have explained in section 2.1.3. Unfortunately, they go further to insist that all human-made capital used in the production of wealth should not be private property either. In my opinion they wrongly conflate the two categories of, land and capital (as defined in this book) into a single entity which they call capital.

Their basis for wealth distribution is 'From each according to his ability; to each according to his needs'. They essentially require everyone to be angels who are willing to share the results of their work and skills with everyone else. I don't think we're quite there yet.

3.2.5   Single-issue parties

There are a few single-issue parties which have very little to say about the fair distribution of wealth and focus instead on issues such as immigration (UKIP).

UKIP sees the wealth distribution problem in Britain and thinks it can be partly solved by cutting foreign aid. Foreign aid can be viewed as rent that is paid to the poorer parts of the world for the privilege of occupying our own fertile, productive and temperate islands. Other rich countries do the same. UKIP, in its nationalistic fervour, has no understanding of this.

The Green Party used to be a single issue party focussed mostly on environmental issues but now their major policies are concerned with a fairer distribution of wealth.

3.3 Housing

People want to own their own homes because doing so enables them to lessen the extent of their slavery. They can stop paying rent to a landlord and avoid the dreadful feeling each year when the landlord raises the rent. They become freeholders of land, and finally, once the mortgage has been paid off, will owe nothing to anyone except a small amount of annual council tax.

However, when a homeowner first purchases a house they are not totally out of slavery, because they become a slave to the mortgage lenders who are charging them interest on their mortgage. The mortgagees must hand over some of their wealth to the landowners who supply the money for the loan.

There are two elements of a house. The first is the land – in other words, the plot that the house occupies. As was argued earlier, this land rightly belongs to society. This means that the owner of a house is today effectively handling stolen goods. They have bought their land from someone who, somewhere further back along the chain of ownership, ultimately stole it from society.

As has been explained in earlier sections, the freehold system means that landowners are able to maintain a scarcity of land which always forces the price of housing land to the maximum price that people are able to pay. The scarcity of houses means that houses are effectively auctioned so as to achieve the highest price that people are able to afford. The seller puts their house on the market at a higher asking price than they think it is worth, encouraged by estate agents who are normally paid a percentage of the selling price. The seller then waits for the highest bidder. The bidders will offer the highest price they can afford in order to escape the slavery of paying a private landlord. To achieve this the bidders will consider cutting many of the things that they would normally enjoy, such as holidays, meals out etc.

The second element of a house is the bricks-and-mortar component. The price of this stays fairly constant, varying only with normal inflation.

It is estimated that on average, two thirds of the price of a house is the land, and the remaining third is the 'bricks and mortar'. This ratio will vary over the country. In London, the land might be worth 95% of the value of the house. Somewhere less economically successful, the land might be worth only 5% of the value of the house.

Hundreds of thousands of homes are left empty, often because owners have inherited them and cannot afford to repair them adequately in order to let them out to tenants. Other houses or flats are bought on a buy-to-leave basis as purely an investment.

Their ownership of housing land causes people to be very sensitive to anything that might affect the value of their bit of land. For example, they may object to planning permission being granted for low-cost social housing in their area because it could cause the value of the land under their (more expensive) houses to fall.

3.4 Women

Women have battled over the last two centuries to achieve equal legal rights with men. They have achieved a lot, yet there are still problems. Margaret Thatcher, the former Conservative Prime Minister, famously joked that "To get to the top, a woman must be twice as good as a man. Fortunately, this is not difficult".

Well, it does seem to be difficult for a lot of women. Women still get paid less than men, and they occupy far fewer senior positions in commerce and government.

Just 5% of the chief executives of FTSE 100 companies in Britain are female, and 20% of small and medium-sized companies are female-led[27]. According to a report published by the London School of Economics, there are very few women among the richest people in the UK and other OECD countries. Out of the wealthiest 53,000 people in the UK in 2013, only 9% were women[28].

There is an explanation for this. Although women now have equal rights in law, the majority of that minority of the population which owns Britain's land are men. It is estimated that globally, though women make up 50% of the population, they own only 1% of the land. This is strongly contested as a myth because there is no reliable data to support it, but I would think there is some truth in it. At one time, in Britain land was handed down to the eldest son under a custom known as *primogeniture,* and even today hereditary peerages can only be passed down to men. Using the power that the ownership of land and wealth confers, landowners are in a position to pull strings and influence decisions, and if these men have any prejudice against women, which isn't unheard of, they may favour men over women.

As a result, there exists a hidden downward pressure on women which at the highest levels leads to them occupying fewer senior positions, and which at the lowest level forces them into poverty and sometimes into prostitution.

Such pressures do not only affect women. Prejudices held by the landowning minority and their accomplices can reveal themselves in the form of reduced wages for any gender, race, religion, class or creed.

3.5 Government debt

The majority of government debt that we hear so much about is residual debt that is the result of the unfair distribution of wealth, which in its turn has resulted from the slavery system we live under.

To explain the idea of residual debt, we can imagine a situation involving two people – A and B – on an island. They both grow potatoes on plots of equal size and quality. They both need ten potatoes a day to survive, so over the year they each grow 10 potatoes per day on average.

Now suppose that A has some claim on B's potatoes, because A owns both plots. A charges B rent for the land of 1 potato per day. So A gets 11 potatoes and B 9. There is an unequal distribution of wealth. To survive, B must borrow 1 potato per day from A. So each produces ten potatoes and each consumes 10 potatoes, but a residual, growing debt of one potato per day is accruing in A's favour.

There is no pile of spare potatoes that can be used to repay the debt. And if B starts to increase production by working harder to grow more potatoes to pay off the debt, A can increase the rent to absorb any increase in productivity. The debt of potatoes can never be repaid, and will only grow.

Note that if B embarks on a regime of austerity and tries to live off just 9 potatoes a day, this causes a pile of potatoes to accumulate in A's barn. Sooner or later, A will cut back his work so as to only produce 9 potatoes. This is equivalent to laying off 10% of the workforce – in other words, there is a recession.

Not only does B owe A a rising number of potatoes, but in addition A expects interest to be paid on that debt. Given that there is no way that B can pay back the debt, B will be paying interest on each borrowed potato in perpetuity.

We can apply a parallel of this potato example to our government debt. The landowners extract wealth from the workers to such an extent that the workers cannot even pay for their own health care and their children's education. So the government taxes the landowners and their accomplices to pay for these things, and if these taxes are still not enough to give the slaves what they need or want, then the government borrows from the landowners. The debt to the landowners is never paid back, but merely rises every year, with few exceptions[29]. The ratio of debt to GDP may rise and fall but the debt consistently rises. There's nothing to pay it back with. It is a residual debt resulting from the unfair distribution of wealth. Note also that if the Chancellor introduces austerity by refusing to borrow more and forcing cutbacks in the wealth redistributed to the slaves, the landowners will have to cut back on production (as in the case of the potato growers), thereby causing a recession.

It must be noted further that interest must be paid in perpetuity for anything that the government borrows from the landowners. Even when a schoolbook has long since been thrown away, interest is paid on it for perpetuity.

The only way to prevent rising residual government debt is to have a fairer system of wealth distribution in the first place. This is the reason that lies behind the Conservative Party's inability to change the deficit to a surplus. They insist on reducing taxes for the rich, allowing them to keep even more of the wealth they have stolen from the slaves. The rich cannot spend it fast enough on themselves so they must lend it to others, one of them being the government. If the government stops borrowing from the rich by introducing too many social welfare cuts it will cut consumption by the slaves and there will be a recession. The Conservative Party will forever be pushing into the future the date when the deficit becomes a surplus.

3.6 Factors affecting the price of land

Section 2.1.2 discusses a significant factor that affects the value of land, namely supply and demand. However, there are many other factors, some of which are described in this section.

3.6.1 Planning permission

A major factor in the value of land is the planning permission that society grants in relation to how it is used. A landowner cannot obtain much rent from a tenant farmer on a few acres of grassland if the planning permission granted by society is for farming only. If the landowner applies for a change to the planning permission in order to allow the grassland to be developed for housing, and society grants the change, the tenant farmer can be evicted at the end of the lease and the rent for that land will increase considerably. Or the rent can be capitalised into a single lump sum and sold to a new owner (the capital value of land is usually about 25 years' worth of rent). Either way, the original landowner has become much wealthier with minimal personal effort. They have benefited from society merely agreeing to change the planning permission applicable to that land.

3.6.2 Location

Differences in the degree of advantage accruing from location, fertility or natural resources mean that some places are more desirable than others, thus affecting the value of the land there. We are probably all familiar with the board game Monopoly, and how enormous the rents payable are to the owners of Mayfair compared to the small rents accruing from the ownership of Old Kent Road. Likewise in Britain, the most valuable land one can own lies under the businesses at the centres of our towns and cities, which generate rents that can be thousands of times higher than those fetched by agricultural land. The value of land at the heart of a city increases massively as society invests in the surrounding infrastructure in the form of roads, water and sewage systems, flood defences, electricity and gas networks, railways and railway stations, bus stations, underground trains, high-speed trains, airports, civic buildings, royal palaces, national museums and art galleries, national theatres, national sports arenas, parks, police forces, fire brigades etc. Landowners who own land that lies within such investment zones benefit massively from all this infrastructure, because the rent they can charge for their land rises.

We have only to investigate rents for shops in UK high streets to see this. In 2010 I looked at the annual rents in Bedford for an average-size high-street shop and found them to be approximately £100k. This rent consists of two components, although it will never be found broken out like this:

1. the rent for the land underneath the shop, i.e. the location, which includes the planning permission for the shop,
2. the rent for the building, which is normally owned by the landowner.

It can be readily seen that a £100k annual rent to the landowner will very soon pay off the initial landowner's cost of building the shop premises, which might be only £300k. The rest of the rent, which will be collected each year for many years, is the rent for the location, which is mostly pocketed by the landowner.

With arable farming, the highest-value land will be sites that have good soils and a warm climate. In addition, flat land allows such machinery as combine harvesters to be used effectively. So this type of farming is concentrated in the south and east of Britain. Agriculture uses 69% of Britain's land area, and the Tenant Farmers Association estimates that tenant farmers are responsible for 40% of the total agricultural area of England and Wales[30]. So there is a significant amount of agriculture-derived rent being collected by landowners.

3.6.3   Technology and automation

Technology and automation affect the value of land. For example, if some of the servers in a fast-food shop can be replaced by a computerised ordering system, the landowner can start to raise the rent in order to absorb the decrease in the fast food shop's wage bill. Likewise, if a tenant farmer achieves higher yields thanks to a new fertilizer, the landowner can raise the rent to absorb the additional profits.

This clearly has implications for the future as more and more jobs are replaced by robots. The landowners will become even wealthier, and unless this wealth is more evenly shared with others, social tensions will escalate.

For an interesting way of representing this economic law in microcosm, watch Dave Wetzel's short, inverted Robinson Crusoe story at https://www.youtube.com/watch?v=WDgTikjUpMs.

I like this video because it demonstrates six things:

1. how landowners took the ownership of land – similar to the Enclosure Acts,
2. the state's complicity in the slavery system as lawmakers and law enforcers,
3. how landowners create the illusion of freedom within a system of slavery,
4. how landowners can live off the work of others,
5. in order to create capital, consumption has to be forgone,
6. how increases in wealth production due to improved technology are pocketed by the landowners.

I told a friend about this video, and his comment was that Robinson Crusoe could just wait for a dark night and then club Man Friday and take over the island. The conventional term for such an action is *violent revolution* – which is not something that we want.

3.6.4   Land taxes
Any state taxes on land will reduce the landowners' rents correspondingly – there's nowhere else for them to come

from because wages are always at a minimum. Britain levies a few small taxes on the ownership of land, though none of them are large enough to significantly affect its price. The first tax of these is Stamp Duty, which is an initial charge that is payable when land is purchased. The second is Council Tax, which is applied to the occupants of houses and flats. The third is the Unified Business Rate, which is a tax on the occupants of commercial premises. Inheritance Tax and Capital Gains Tax may also account for a very small amount of taxation on land.

State land taxes can affect the supply of land. Any land left idle which is incurring a state charge will encourage the owner to make it productive, thus increasing its supply and decreasing its value. However, the state charges need to be higher than the amount by which land speculators think their land will increase in value each year, or the speculators might simply sit tight on their unused land.

3.6.5 Taxes

Taxes such as income tax affect the value of land. Given that wages are always pressed down to the lowest possible level, if the government raises income tax there is only one place it can come from – the landowners' rents. Conservative governments always campaign for low taxes for this very reason.

3.6.6 Interest rates

Interest rates affect the amount of interest that businesses pay on their loans. If interest rates are reduced, meaning that companies pay less interest on their debt and so become more profitable, landowners can raise their rents, thereby increasing the value of their land.

Low interest rates allow borrowers to borrow more, also increasing the price of land. In the current low-interest-rate environment, prices for housing land are increasing, which will in turn increase the price of houses.

3.6.7 Government subsidies

The Help to Buy scheme allows lenders to offer higher mortgages to borrowers who have secured government guarantees, enabling the lender to be refunded some of the losses incurred on the mortgage if the borrower defaults on their mortgage repayments. This increases the value of housing land, and consequently increases house prices.

3.7 The Regions

The distribution of the wealth controlled by government across Britain's regions is very unequal.

3.7.1 London

3.7.1.1 Public spending

Consider first the public money that is spent on and in London:

Central government is based there. Many of the 650 MPs rent flats there, which are paid for by public money. Some of their salaries are spent there, as are some of their expenses and allowances. Then there are all the associated buildings to be maintained and serviced, such as Downing Street and the Houses of Parliament. This is all financed from public money that is being disbursed by government into the London economy.

The 800 or so members of the House of Lords spend a good portion of their expenses in London.

There are 24 government ministries which have armies of civil servants to support them, many of which are based in or around London. A good deal of their salaries and expenses flow into the London economy. All their buildings must be maintained and serviced and secured.

The royal family is primarily based in London, where there are related palaces and historic buildings to be maintained, the Civil List to be paid and security maintained, much of the cost of which will be spent in London.

London houses the major national museums, such as the British Museum, the Science Museum, the Natural History Museum, the Victoria and Albert Museum, plus a host of others. Their buildings have to be maintained and serviced, and the salaries of the people who work there have to be paid.

There has been a huge public investment in transport in London. There is an extensive underground system. The main railway lines radiate from London, as do the motorways – one of which, the M25 London Orbital motorway, has been massively expensive to construct and maintain. The country's major airports – Heathrow, Gatwick, London City, Luton and Stansted – are located in the vicinity of London. There is the HS1 (the rail link to the Channel tunnel) and the proposed HS2. Crossrail is almost complete, and another rail line from north London to south London is proposed.

All the major national and international events for most of the popular sports such as football, cricket and rugby (union and league) are held in London, as are the London Marathon, the Boat Race and the Olympics; all these events are supported, policed and secured using public money.

In terms of the arts, the BBC is based there, as are the National Theatre, the English National Opera, the Royal Ballet, the Royal Opera, the Albert Hall, the National Gallery, the Tate Modern, and the Royal Philharmonic Orchestra.

Partly as a result of all this public investment in London, all major companies want to have their headquarters there. Foreign billionaires want to live there. Foreign tourists mostly go to London. Some of them may include a short visit to Oxford and/or Cambridge and Stratford-on-Avon, but most will spend their money in London. This greatly benefits the powerful London landowners because it increases the rents they can charge, and forcing both wages and taxes down enables them to pocket the surplus.

3.7.1.2   Finance industry

London is one of the largest centres of global finance. The world's landowners love to park their gains from slavery in London for two main reasons.

The first is that Britain is a powerful island that is not easily invaded. In fact, it has not been successfully invaded for nearly a thousand years. So people feel very safe depositing their money there.

The second reason is that London's finance industry sits at the centre of a network of British-run tax havens such as the Cayman Islands, Jersey, Bermuda, the British Virgin Islands and the Isle of Man. This allows the world's landowners and their accomplices to deposit their money in London and to have it shifted by specialist banks and accountancy firms into the tax havens.

The flow of money through London is a big generator of wealth for Britain, but most of it goes to the London-based finance industry.

3.7.1.3 Location

Land is more valuable if it is located close to its markets because its proximity to them reduces transport costs. Britain's largest export market is Europe, so London and the south-east in general are well placed to take advantage of this geographical closeness. This is one of the reasons that the population is gradually moving there.

The rents in London are consequently very high compared to the rest of the country, and as I explained in section 3.1.2, the tax system fails to capture the full rental value of the land, with the result that London landowners are even wealthier than they should be.

People like to hear that their capital is the most dynamic and vibrant city in the world, especially those who live there. However, their pride comes at the expense of downgrading the rest of the country.

3.7.2 The other regions of Britain

Section 3.1.2 on income tax explains how the current tax system advantages land with a high rental value, because it allows the landowner to take more of the extra income that good-quality sites generate.

Businesses in the regions are generally situated on worse-quality sites than those in the southeast. Since they are further from EU markets, they do not benefit as much as London from public spending, and they do not benefit as much from the wealth that flows to the finance industry. And because the tax system hits worse-quality sites harder, the other regions always suffer first in a recession, which is why they are always poorer and experience greater levels of unemployment. The government has tried to compensate for this phenomenon by setting up regional development funds, but this in no way makes up for the unfairness of the tax system.

3.8 The greatest of these is rent

Earlier, this book covered the three income streams that the landowners receive from businesses, namely: rent for land and buildings, interest on debt, and a share of the profits in the form of dividends. However, for the landowner the most important of the three income streams is rent.

The rent that businesses pay to landowners is largely hidden. One cannot inspect a company's accounts and identify the rent or lease items. These are always grouped with other expenses, whereas the interest paid on debt is always visible, as is the amount paid out in dividends.

Landowners do not approve of businesses complaining about their rents to the media, and CEOs are too well paid as accomplices to betray their landowners. If businesses did complain they could be blacklisted and denied future access to premises for their business.

Rental contracts usually have a clause that allows the rent to be increased by a specified percentage each year. This is the way that landowners absorb any improvements in the process of wealth production. As society develops improved technologies that lead to higher productivity, the aim of the landowners is to take all those improvements for themselves while keeping the slaves' wages constant. And this is exactly what we find in most surveys of wealth. The landowners and their accomplices get richer, whereas the wealth of the poor either stays at the same level or worsens. Again, this is achieved through the primary rule of economics that applies when all the land is owned: wages are always forced down to the minimum, leaving the increased surplus to be absorbed by the landowners.

When financial analysts talk about who is entitled to what when a company goes into bankruptcy, they usually mention a hierarchy of rights. At the top, they say, are secured bond holders, i.e. those who lent money to the company with the guarantee that if the company could not repay it they would either get specified capital belonging to the company (such as machinery and stockpiles) or the monies realized from the sale of that capital. Next in line are any unsecured bond holders who lent money to the company, trusting that the company would be able to repay it. Lowest in the hierarchy of rights are the shareholders, who get a share of what is left – if there is anything at all.

However, these financial analysts tend not to mention people or organisations that become creditors to the company after it has declared bankruptcy. Such creditors are given the highest priority in terms of debt repayment, even over the secured bond holders, so that the company can continue to trade and obtain credit from its suppliers even after seeking bankruptcy.

Rent would fall into this category because a rent bill is presented periodically, so if it is presented after the company has filed for bankruptcy it will be assigned the highest priority.

3.9 Stability of the economy

The 2008-9 financial crisis was largely caused by a crash in the inflated price of houses, causing some mortgage lending banks to require bailouts from the government. This resulted in a credit crunch which produced a recession, because trade relies on being able to obtain credit for transactions.

When I say 'a crash in the price of houses', I really mean a crash in the value of the land underneath the houses. The price of bricks and mortar is reasonably constant, give or take a bit of retail price inflation. But the price of the land underneath those houses can vary a great deal. A house in London may be worth £2 million, but if the same house was transplanted to Hartlepool, say, its value would be considerably less. It is the value of the land – the location – that is different.

Effectively, the price of land has a net present value (NPV) of infinity if it can be handed down generation after generation, which is what happens to a lot of land. The only limit on the price of land is the amount of money people have with which to buy it, or the size of the debt that people are allowed to take on in order to do so. That is why mortgage debt becomes more affordable when interest rates are reduced: people take on higher mortgages, and so the price of housing land rises. Similarly, if the lenders relax their rules on the salary multiples that people are allowed to borrow on when they take out a mortgage, the price of housing land rises. If government provides subsidies for buying land, e.g. 'Help to Buy', the price of housing land rises. Governments are completely ignorant if they believe they are helping first-time buyers by giving them subsidies. All they are doing is increasing the price of housing land, and so the first-time buyers are no better off.

If people had to pay rent to society for the land their homes occupy, the price of houses would be massively cheaper. The price would simply be the price of the construction materials and the labour required to build them. People might baulk at the idea of always paying rent, but they are effectively already paying rent to the landowners in the form of the interest on their mortgage debt.

3.10 Class system
According to Oxfam, the 85 richest people in the world now control as much wealth as the poorest half of the global population put together. "Widening inequality is creating a vicious circle where wealth and power are increasingly concentrated in the hands of a few, leaving the rest of us to fight over crumbs from the top table," says the charity's executive director.

Such wealth inequality produces a class system: a system where those at the top enjoy more wealth than they know what to do with and conduct themselves with a false feeling of confidence and superiority over those below them, while those at the bottom have just enough to live on and experience an unjustified sense of inadequacy and inferiority.

Royalty are the apex of this class system, followed by the aristocracy, lesser land owners and senior accomplices.

Poorer people suffer from a wide array of health problems as a result of their unfavourable economic status. They are unable to take advantage of health care as often as the wealthy; and when they do do so it is usually of worse quality, even though they tend to develop health problems at a much higher rate. Poorer families have greater rates of infant mortality, cancer, cardiovascular disease, and disabling physical injuries. Additionally, poor people tend to work in much more hazardous conditions, yet they generally have much less (or no) health insurance provided for them compared to middle- and upper-class workers.

3.11 The Establishment and the Elite

The Establishment consists of two groups of people: the landowners, and their senior accomplices. The landowners are the hidden, anonymous group, the non-visible part of the establishment, who are able to pull strings using their money and influence. They generally live off rent gained from inherited land.

Their senior accomplices make up what we know as the 'elite'. They are the visible part of the establishment. They are the senior politicians, CEOs, the top brass of the armed services, bankers, and the heads of universities and colleges (especially Oxbridge). The elite are genuinely intelligent and capable – that's how they became the elite. But they dance to the tune of the landowners.

3.12 Education

The education system in Britain is distorted by the unfair distribution of wealth caused by the MBSS.

In general, the landowners and their accomplices can afford to send their children to private schools (sometimes confusingly called 'public schools') that can offer them a better education, because these schools have the money they obtain from fees to pay for better facilities and better teachers. The slaves send their children to state schools because they can't afford private schools. Britain's private schools, which can mostly be afforded by the rich only, are subsidised to the tune of £700 million a year due to their charitable status. As one *Guardian* journalist said, "We might as well subsidise five-star hotels." [31]

If a comprehensive school develops a good reputation, the house prices around it will rise because those who can afford to do so move into the area in order to enable their children to take advantage of what it offers. The result is that only wealthier people are able to send their children to a comprehensive school with a good reputation.

Wealthier people who can afford private tutors for their 11-year-olds are more likely to get them through a grammar-school entrance exam.

Seven per cent of Britain's pupils attend private schools, and yet they take up approximately 41% of the places at the prestigious of Oxford University and Cambridge University.[32] Why is it that landowners want to send their children there? The reason is that those two universities are superior in many ways. And why are they superior? It is simply because these universities and their colleges have a lot of something that other universities and colleges have much less of – land. There are many (possibly mythical) stories, such as the alleged fact that it is possible to walk from Oxford to Cambridge without leaving university-owned land. According to a disclosure which Merton College, Oxford very reluctantly supplied, Merton College owns 134,447 acres of agricultural land, 74 commercial properties and 50 residential properties. [33] That's just one of the Oxford colleges. The university itself also owns land. Then there is Cambridge University and its colleges.

With the rental income from their land, these universities have been able to build a portfolio of other assets, such as shares and bonds. And with the income from this portfolio they are able to provide their students with a superior educational experience. This superiority is not visible in the form of a few individual large things, but rather in a hundred lesser things. Examples are:

- grade 1 listed buildings that are prestigious, historic and expensive to maintain,
- the tutorial system, which requires more teaching than at other universities,
- money in the form of scholarships and exhibitions awarded in order to attract the brightest students
- professors who are paid more than at other universities[34],

- other academic staff who are paid more than at other universities,
- college fellows enjoying chef-prepared dinners at High Table plus wine from the college wine cellar,
- each college having its own or shared boathouse for its rowing boats,
- each college having its own or shared rugby/soccer/cricket/athletic fields and facilities,
- the university also having its own well-equipped sporting facilities,
- each faculty of the university having state-of-the-art facilities,
- Oxford University having five major museums,
- Oxford University having the Bodleian library, one of the six legal deposit libraries in the country,
- some colleges having their own punting facilities
- free reunion dinners for college alumni.

Another source of income for the two universities comes from their (frequently rich) alumni, who often bequeath some of their wealth to the colleges. Colleges regularly hold free dinners for any alumni who have promised the college money in their wills.

Also, because of their prestige, the universities attract millions of tourists and conferences, both of which provide additional income.

These wealthy universities try to distract everyone from their privileged status by emphasising their focus on increasing the percentage of state school-educated pupils. However, that focus doesn't solve the problem; it merely results in more state school-educated students enjoying the privileges that accrue from studying at Oxbridge, and being seduced by the idea that such privilege is acceptable and something to be sought further in the MBSS.

I don't have any problem with the people at these universities – the ones I have met are generally very nice. But these universities are a big cog in the slavery system.

3.13 Social mobility

People may move up or down the social ladder within their own lifetime, or from one generation to the next. The notion that everyone should have the same chance of moving up is what lies behind the concept of equality of opportunity.

One way to measure social mobility is to see whether rich parents have rich children and poor parents have poor children, or whether the incomes of parents and their children are unrelated. Can the children of poor parents become rich? Researchers at the London School of Economics have used this measure to compare social mobility in eight European and North American countries. Their data shows that at least among these few countries, the more equal countries have higher social mobility. [35]

Greater inequalities of outcome seem to make it easier for rich parents to pass on their advantages. As income differences have widened in Britain, so social mobility has slowed. Bigger income differences may make it harder to achieve equality of opportunity because they increase social class differentiation, and possibly prejudice.

3.14 Public projects

The private ownership of land creates huge problems for public projects. As soon as the government announces a public project, such as HS2 (the high-speed rail link from London to the Midlands and the North) or Heathrow's third runway, the affected landowners start assessing the impact it will have on the value of their land, and then either rub their hands with glee at the increased rent they will get if the project raises the value of their land, or start arguing for a cancellation of the project (or at least significant compensation) because they claim that the value of their land will be adversely affected by the project.

Public projects should be assessed in terms of the net increase of wealth production they generate, and should be funded by the increase in rent that society will receive for the land affected by this project.

Let us take the third runway for Heathrow as an example. The runway might result in a reduction in the rent value of the housing land located under the flight path serving the runway, but it would result in an increase in the value of the land for the airport and for the businesses based around the airport, possibly extending well out of the immediate area. For society, the project should be successful if it results in a net increase in the value of the land rent.

3.15 Globalism

The globalisation of markets is simply slavery on an international scale. It represents money that is seeking to exploit slave labour which possesses the right skills in the right location. This is not a new phenomenon – the investment made by British landowners in sugar plantations in the 17th century was an example of globalism. With the improved communications brought by the internet and the ability of money to move around the globe overnight, globalism has become a much more prominent aspect of business life.

Globalism is very beneficial for landowners and their accomplices. It introduces competition between countries in attracting businesses by offering a low-tax environment. We often hear about countries wishing to reduce corporation tax in order to attract businesses.

Globalism offers landowners and their political wing, the Conservative Party, a great argument for keeping income taxes low, because otherwise the most skilled accomplices will move to a country with lower income taxes, resulting in less wealth for Britain.

And as the book explains in section 3.1.2, the lower the taxes, the richer are the landowners and their accomplices. The downward drive on taxation is contributing to making the landowners and their accomplices ever wealthier. As their wealth grows, so does their power to influence policy. All of the progress made by socialist governments in achieving a fairer distribution of wealth is being slowly nibbled away by the Conservative government on behalf of the landowners and their accomplices – starting with the weakest in society.

3.16 Wildlife

The concentration of land ownership in the uplands of Britain has allowed landowners to deforest upland Britain in order to facilitate their sports of grouse shooting and deer stalking. This deforestation is largely maintained by sheep and deer farming, and by rotational burning on grouse moors that produces a near-monoculture of heather. This has resulted in reduced number of species, increased flooding risks, and monocultures of wildlife. (See George Monbiot's article on this subject [36]).

3.17 Brexit

Brexit, like everything else, is primarily about the MBSS. The Brexit move has come from the Conservative Party who believe that they have lost too much control of the slavery system. They believe that under the dominance of more socialist countries like Germany and France the EU has allowed too much wealth to be given to the slaves, including paid annual leave, time off for antenatal appointments and fair treatment for part-time workers. The landowners and their accomplices, using their political wing – the Conservative Party – would like to retake control of the slavery system and slowly reclaim all the wealth that has been given away.

Of course this goal is rarely mentioned; instead, there is a smokescreen of confusion which has even got the slaves voting to have their rights taken away in a "turkeys voting for Christmas" manner.

4 Problems with the MBSS

This section discusses the problems created by the Modern British Slavery System.

The MBSS can be characterised as a set of plantations which covers the whole of Britain. The slaves have the freedom to move from one plantation to another, but they will find similar conditions on all of them. Their wages are forced down to the minimum, and they are working mostly to make the landowners and their accomplices richer.

The slaves are able to democratically vote for a new government, but they cannot vote for a new set of owners. The owners are continually exerting their power and influence over the government, so it matters little who the slaves vote for. They are still caught in a slavery system and stigmatised for any wealth transfers they receive from the government.

The slaves are forced to participate in a rat race in which they work within the context of a so-called meritocracy that is actually just an embedded component of the wider slavery system.

4.1 Disturbance of the peace

The main problem with the MBSS is that it produces an unfair distribution of wealth, which in turn causes a disturbance of the peace. Specifically, it disturbs the internal peace of people's minds, which can then lead to an external disturbance of the peace. We know that people can be happy with very little, as long as everybody else has very little. However, the existence of large differences in wealth without good reason causes disturbances. The types of disturbance they cause are:

- divisions between the various strata of society, and a lack of unity. This is the complete opposite of the mantras recited by the promoters of 'one-nation Conservatism',
- resentment of privilege,
- resentment at having to work hard for very little pay
- unwarranted pride on the part of those who own land, and unwarranted humility on the part of those who don't,
- class hatred,
- fear of land losing its value,
- fawning by those looking to ingratiate themselves with the landowners and their accomplices,
- anger. A criticism often levelled at left-wingers is that they get so angry and violent. The reason for their anger is clear. What belongs to them by right – land – has been stolen from them in the past, often by force,
- the frustration of knowing that something is wrong, but not being able to identify its cause,
- confusion caused by the complex tax system we live under, and the inefficiency it produces
- hopelessness and despair when faced with the prospect of a life of slavery,
- guilt when failing to declare a cash income in tax returns, and also guilt in those who are fully aware that they are participating in criminal tax fraud.

A slavery system turns people against each other. It poisons their relationships.

4.2 Slavery

This book has described a system of slavery in Britain. In these enlightened times slavery is considered to be abhorrent, and yet here we find ourselves in the midst of a system of slavery.

Some people have more wealth than they can use, while others are having to take several low-paid jobs and work all hours just to get by. Some people, such as cleaners, may have to spend many hours a day travelling to those low-paid jobs because they cannot afford to live near their work.

4.3 Poverty

The phrase 'the working poor' is increasingly in use. Over half of the UK's poor live in households that contain at least one working adult.

Six million people earn less than the hourly national living wage, which is currently defined as £9.15 in London and £7.85 in the rest of the UK.

This is a symptom of the MBSS which forces down wages to subsistence levels.

4.4 Theft

Landowners are charging rent for much of the land that they have stolen from society. The greatest degree of theft is occurring in our towns and cities, where society has invested public money which makes the privately owned land more valuable. Landowners are social scroungers on a massive scale.

4.5 Inefficiency

The simplest way to raise money for communal projects is for society to charge rent to those people who use what belongs to society. This is not a tax, but simply a payment in return for the use of something that doesn't belong exclusively to the user. This would be a very easy system to administer, and the rent would be very difficult to avoid paying.

The landowners and their accomplices do not want this simple system because they are richer under the slavery system. So in order to avoid paying a fair rent for what they use, instead we have a massively complex, unfair and loophole-ridden tax system. Governments spend most of their time devising tweaks to this massively complex system and arguing about these tweaks with the Opposition.

There is an army of civil servants whose job is to implement these tweaks and try to make them work, while a parallel army of accountants working for companies and rich individuals is helping its respective clients to exploit the tax loopholes.

Wealth is being stolen from the slaves. Some of it is recouped from the landowners and their accomplices through the tax system and then redistributed to the slaves. This is a very inefficient way of distributing wealth.

4.6 Demotivation

People become demotivated if they think they are working hard mainly in order to make someone else rich. Demotivation leads to a reduced enjoyment of life and reduced productivity.

Six in 10 employees told a survey by the Chartered Institute of Personnel and Development (CIPD) that the high level of chief executives' pay discouraged them in the workplace, and more than half of those surveyed felt that such a high level of pay was bad for a firm's reputation.

"The growing disparity between pay at the high and lower ends of the pay scale for today's workforce is leading to a real sense of unfairness, which is impacting on employees' motivation at work," said Charles Cotton, CIPD's reward adviser.

4.7 Debt

When a small minority have more wealth than it can use, there are only two possible outcomes. Their wealth either has to be lent to others, building an ever-increasing debt mountain that will one day collapse, or the production of wealth will stop, causing a recession. It would be preferable to share this wealth more fairly, in order to avoid either alternative having to be faced.

4 Problems with the MBSS

5 Potential Solutions

Previous sections have analysed the workings of the MBSS and the problems it causes. This section discusses possible solutions to the problems caused by the MBSS that have been identified here, and recommends one of them for further consideration in section 6.

5.1 Land rent

Ultimately, there is only one fair way to run an economy, and that is not to have any taxes, but instead to have people pay rent for anything they use that doesn't belong to them, especially land. If people want to use society's land, they should pay a rent to society for the privilege. This is the option recommend for further consideration in section 6.

5.2 Higher minimum wage

One way to achieve a fairer distribution of wealth would be to leave the current slavery system in place, but increase the legal national minimum wage.

The mean annual wage at the moment is about £31,800 (2014-15). A minimum wage for unskilled labour could be set at, say, £25,000 for everyone aged over 18. Wages for skilled work would then be forced to rise in order to maintain the differentials.

Companies would not be able to remain solvent with these wage rises unless they drastically cut the rent they paid to the landowners, as well as the level of pay given to their currently overcompensated managers and other accomplices. This would result in a fairer distribution of wealth.

Landowners would fight back by not accepting reduced rents and forcing companies into bankruptcy, creating unemployment and general chaos and confusion, in the hope that the change would be withdrawn. However, in the long run they would have to accept lower rents and lower wages for their accomplices.

The other way that landowners would fight back would be to seek the reduction of all secondary distributions of wealth (the National Health Service, state education, tax credits, housing benefit etc) so that their own taxes could be reduced.

This would go some way towards a fairer distribution of wealth. However, the mechanics of the slavery system would all still be in place, with the new system of wealth distribution being precariously dependent on the guaranteed wage law, which would be continuously opposed and campaigned against.

5.3   Universal Basic Wage

A Universal Basic Wage would involve the government giving each adult, say, £12,000 per year irrespective of whether that adult worked or not. Any wage an adult obtained from work would be in addition to the guaranteed wage received from the government. Most forms of social benefits could then be removed, saving all the administration that goes with them.

If the net result was an increase in government spending because the cost of the guaranteed wage was greater than the savings in social benefits, one would have to ask where the extra money would have to come from. It would only make sense for the government to increase the taxes on the rich to pay for this additional expenditure.

Note that if a guaranteed wage was introduced, the government would be obliged to retain the minimum-wage legislation. If not, companies would be at liberty to drastically reduce the wages they paid to low-skilled workers (in accordance with the dynamics of the fundamental economic law described in section 2.2), meaning that low-skilled workers would be no better off overall, and the government-guaranteed wage would effectively be paid to businesses instead of to workers.

Note also that if the guaranteed wage resulted in low-skilled workers being better off, the dynamic nature of the slavery system would cause rents and house prices to rise to a level where those workers were no better off than they were previously.

5.4   Increased taxes on the rich

A fairer distribution of wealth could be achieved by increasing taxes on the rich. This is one of the strategies of Britain's socialists, along with a national minimum wage. This strategy leaves the slavery system in place but raises taxes on the landowners and their accomplices, and redistributes the revenue from taxes to the slaves in the form of welfare payments.

Unfortunately, this strategy is very hard to implement successfully. There are many loopholes in Britain's complex tax system that allow the rich to avoid paying taxes. They can move their money and assets into trust funds, or keep their money offshore.

The other argument used against this approach is that successful entrepreneurs might want to move to another part of the globe where slavery systems which they could take advantage of are still in place.

5.5   Land redistribution

Land redistribution involves sharing out the land fairly so that all of us benefit from land ownership, and not just a few, thus producing a fairer distribution of wealth. One hears of this being tried in other countries, such as in southern Africa. However, this approach is mostly applied to undeveloped agricultural land.

There are 60 million acres in Britain and 66 million people, so each person could have just under one acre. Or each family could have two acres.

There are many problems with this approach. One is that a single acre of Mayfair is worth a lot more than an acre of moorland. So does one person get, say, a tenth of an acre of Mayfair while another gets a thousand acres of moorland?

Would people or organisations get the land for free? Would they get the land in perpetuity, or just for life, i.e. could they hand it down to their children? If the population expands, does everybody's plot have to be reduced in order to create more plots, and vice versa? Would we have to return to an economy in which most people are small-scale farmers?

Clearly, this solution would generate many more problems than it might solve.

5.6 Communism

Communism attempts to create a fairer distribution of wealth by putting all the means of production – land, capital and people's work – in the hands of the state, and distributing the resulting wealth. The basis of the wealth distribution is the principle of 'from each according to his abilities; to each according to his needs'. But how do we define what people's needs are? Our needs always seem to be greater than what's available, no matter how much of it there is.

I can understand how communism could work if none of us ever thought of our own selfish needs, and only consider the benefit of all. Unfortunately, this requires us to be saints, and I don't see much evidence of that at the moment.

Communism also favours a heavy income tax, which, as section 3.1.2 explains, is a very unfair tax because it takes no account of the value of the land on which the income is generated.

Communists also doesn't permit inheritance. I believe that once people have created wealth they should be able to do what they like with it, free of tax. It is obviously the inheritance of *land* that I disagree with.

5 Potential Solutions

6 Proposed Solution

This section proposes a new system to solve the problems identified so far in this book, and outlines what the benefits of this solution would be.

We are each born into a sort of personal slavery. As we become adults we have a choice – to work as a slave to support ourselves, or to die. For example, if someone is alone on an island and they do not work to get food, shelter and fuel, they will perish. Likewise in our society, if nobody works there will be no food, fuel, shelter, etc. We are obliged to work to enable us to stay alive. The question then is: given that work has to be done, what is the fairest way to organise it?

In my view, the fairest way is certainly not to allow a small number of people to take possession of the earth's natural resources on which we all depend, to charge rent for their use, and to treat the people who work on that land as slaves – which is the system we have now. Surely a much fairer system would give society ownership of the land, and then anybody who wanted to use it would pay rent to society. This rent would provide a natural fund for common needs like roads, justice, defence, looking after those who were unable to look after themselves, etc.

This book has argued that we live in a system based on slavery, and that the control over people that allows the slavery system to exist derives from the fact that all commercial land is owned by a minority of individuals.

To get rid of this control over people, and hence eliminate the system of slavery, it is necessary to abolish the ownership of land. Instead, any person or any organisation who wishes to occupy or have control of a given portion of land should pay to society the rent that society decides the land comprising the rented site is worth. This source of revenue would replace the current need for an unfair, artificial, massively complex and inefficient tax system.

Many people have put a lot of thought into how a land rent-based system of wealth distribution would operate, so I will not go into a lot of detail but will merely outline the main features.

6.1 Tenets of the new system

The two fundamental tenets of the new system are:

1. anything not made by humans – i.e. land as defined in section 2.1.1 – belongs to society. People or organisations who want to use society's land must pay the assessed rent for the privilege,

2. anything human-made – wealth as defined in section 2.1.9 – belongs to the people or organisations who produced it. They are free to consume it, sell it or rent it to someone else without incurring any taxation.

6.2 Main features of the new system

The main features of the new system would be:

6.2.1 Land Registry

All land in all its forms (agricultural land, moorland, land under houses, land under businesses, parkland, forests, mineral deposits such as oil, coal, iron, copper etc, lakes, rivers, the air, the airwaves and sunshine etc), would be registered in the Land Registry.

Society would have free access to the Land Registry information.

6.2.2   Land tenure

All land would belong to a 'societal entity' in a manner similar to that under which it is currently owned by the Crown. The nature of the 'societal entity' would need to be agreed. It could, for example, be a republic.

The current freehold system of land tenure from the Crown would be abolished and replaced with a land rental system.

Other than the wages a person or individual could obtain from land, land would be worth nothing to an individual or organization, because they would be obliged to pay society the full rent value of that land, from which society would benefit correspondingly.

6.2.3   Wealth

All wealth, i.e. anything made by humans, would belong to those who produced it or those they might subsequently have sold it to. This would clearly include all houses, flats and commercial premises.

6.2.4   Capital

It was previously discussed how, in order to create capital, some consumption has to be forgone. For example, if somebody wants to start growing potatoes in their back garden they will need to provide a spade (i.e. the capital needed for growing potatoes), and may need to make some sacrifices to afford it.

Under the proposed new system, it is important for wealth generation that all wages should not be frittered away merely on consumption. Therefore it is proposed that part of the land rent would be allocated to creating a pool of society-owned capital. People or organisations would be able to borrow from this pool at interest in order to purchase capital. Once the loan was paid off, this capital would become the property of the people/organisation.

The result would be that the interest on the capital would go to society rather than to landowners, and that the system would conform to the second fundamental tenet – that all human-made wealth belongs to the people who made it. This is in contrast to Marxism, which proposes that all capital – 'the means of production' – would belong to society.

6.2.5   Planning permission

Just as now, society would be in control of planning permission. So, for example, it would not be permissible to convert a house to a shop without planning permission. Society would be able to grant adequate land for housing. Society would also decide what land should be reserved for public facilities such as parks and public services.

6.2.6   Land rent assessment

Each land site would be regularly rent-assessed by professional surveyors. The rent would reflect the value of the site, including whatever planning permission it came with. It would not include the value of any buildings erected on that site, because they would belong to whoever built them or to whoever they might subsequently have been sold.

The rent would be assessed with reference to a marginal site for the same activity – a site where it is only just possible to make a decent living. Marginal sites would pay no rent, and better sites would pay a correspondingly higher rent.

The land rent charged could be seen as a mechanism for neutralizing or equalising the effect of location on a business. With the effect of location taken out of wealth distribution, the only differentiators between what people earned would be the amount of skill and effort they put into the business – a true meritocracy.

Take a newsagents shop as an example. On the very edge of town it is not possible to make a living as a newsagent, even without land rent, because there is little footfall. Further into town, the footfall increases to a point where there is enough revenue from sales to make a living as long as there is no land rent. This is the marginal site, and no land rent would be payable. Moving into the centre of town, the newsagent would achieve progressively more revenue from the sales arising from the increased footfall. This would be reflected in the land rent, so that the newsagent in the centre of town would make no more profit than the newsagent located on the marginal site.

Rent for sites used for mineral extraction would reflect the volume of minerals extracted as well as the location and difficulty of extraction.

Houses would have their land rent assessed in a similar way. A major factor in the value of the land under a house is its proximity to employment. Unfortunately, a factor that currently seems to be more dominant is the beauty of its location. Our distorted wealth distribution system means that there are people with so much money that they are able to compete with each other on price in order to buy second homes in beautiful locations like national parks and the coast – places that are often far away from lucrative employment. Any local people who need to live and work in such places are priced out of the market.

Under a fairer system of wealth distribution, fewer people would be able to pay the full land rent for second homes. This would mean that houses would become available at a reasonable price to people who need live and work in such places, rather than the situation forcing them out as they currently are.

Changes in planning permission could cause the land rent for the site and any other affected sites to be reassessed. Similarly, public infrastructure developments such as roads, railways and airport runways could cause land rent on nearby sites to be reassessed either upwards or downwards, depending on the impact of the development in question.

Information about the assessed rent for all sites would be freely available to the public.

6.2.7   Rental contracts

People or organisations would take out a rental contract with society for any land they wished to occupy. The contract would specify the planning permission, the land rent and a defined period of security of tenure, which could normally be extended at the end of that period, plus any existing rights of way that others might have over the site, such as public footpaths. The contract would specify that the land would have to be returned in the condition it was in at the beginning of the tenure period. During the period of the contract the renter would have exclusive use of the site.

Having paid the land rent, people and organisations would be free to keep or trade any wealth they had created, free of tax.

6.2.8   Land improvements

Two transactions would be involved in taking occupation of land. One is taking on the land rental contract described above. The second is the buying from the existing owner of all the improvements, if any, on a site, for example the house, swimming pool, garden wall etc. The owner of the improvements or planned improvements is always the one who is liable for the land rent.

6.2.9   Use of land rent

The land rent paid to society would be used for communal projects and needs. It would be distributed on a national, regional and local basis.

Those unable to work because they were too young, too old or too sick would be looked after using the money from land rent.

Foreign aid would still be distributed to poorer countries. This would be considered as Britain's collective payment of land rent for the privilege of living on these fertile and temperate islands.

6.2.10 Land consumption

Industries that consume the earth's resources, such as mining, quarrying, oil and gas extraction, would also incur a charge based on the amount of the land consumed.

6.3 Benefits of the new system

The benefits of the new system would be:

The introduction of land rent would cause people and organisations to reconsider whether they could still afford to occupy or have control over the land they were in charge of. Land that is not used to its full value, and which attracts land rent, would be given up in order to avoid incurring rent liability, so more land would become available. There would be an end to land scarcity and land speculation.

There are supposedly hundreds of thousands of unoccupied homes in Britain. Their owners would usually give them up rather than pay the land rent for them. Many second homes would also be given up, because few people would want to pay the full land rent for land that cannot be passed down as an inheritance. Homes would become available to local people, who would therefore no longer be priced out of their local area.

The wages of workers would rise, because nobody would work for less than they could make by working for themselves on unoccupied land. Wages would rise at the expense of rent, interest and dividends paid to landowners, and at the expense of the wages paid to overcompensated accomplices. The current system of slavery would end.

In the same way that land would not be worth owning, companies would not be worth owning either, because the wealth the company would generate would go to the workers in the form of wages. As a consequence, the stock market would largely disappear. The concept of profit would largely disappear – there would only be wages.

The wage structure would become that of a much purer meritocracy based on skill and effort. The difference between the lowest wage and the highest wage would be much smaller than it is now. Work would be a lot more collaborative without a 'them' and 'us' approach. Wealth distribution would be a great deal fairer, being based purely on merit. As the result of this much fairer distribution of wealth, relations between people would become considerably more harmonious.

The power of landowners and their accomplices to exercise any prejudices they might harbour on the basis of gender, creed, race or class would disappear.

Privilege and the class system would disappear. Privileged private healthcare and private education would decrease dramatically, with a corresponding improvement in the condition of state education and the NHS. The privileged position of Oxford and Cambridge universities would disappear, along with the 'old boy' network.

House prices would be a lot lower, because buyers would only be paying upfront for the bricks-and-mortar component.

The finance sector would shrink, because no mortgages would need to be taken out in order to pay for the capital value of land.

Politics would change. There would be no 'left' and 'right'. The concept of political parties arguing over distribution of wealth would largely disappear.

Public infrastructure projects would be a lot easier to achieve, so the infrastructure all over Britain would improve dramatically.

The fear of automation destroying jobs would no longer be a problem, because the additional wealth created by automation would be collected via land rent and shared by all.

Unemployment would be greatly reduced, because there would always be land at the margin that people could rent for free.

The state would shrink, because there would be a lot less need for the redistribution of wealth. HMRC would become a lot smaller, because collecting a single rent payment is far simpler than administering a complex tax system. Fewer civil servants would be needed.

Governments would no longer get into debt trying to redistribute wealth from the rich to the poor.

The regions would be more prosperous, because they would no longer be severely penalised by the unfairness of the current income tax and VAT arrangements. They would also receive more of the public investment that is currently lavished on London.

There would be less focus on London and the southeast, because the land rents there would be much higher, inducing people to seek lower land rents elsewhere in the country.

Paying rent for the use of land provides a mechanism for preventing abuse of the earth – a green solution. Companies are currently able to pollute the natural resources which belong to society without paying the true cost of such things as air pollution and rubbish that is dumped into the sea.

People's motivation would increase enormously, because they would retain the true value of their work rather than making somebody else rich. The quality of work would improve all round.

Fairer wealth distribution would result in reduced levels of personal debt and a more stable economy.

People would no longer get rich simply as a result of changes to planning permission, e.g. for building houses on agricultural land.

There would be no need for the current totalitarian practice of forcing everyone to reveal their financial affairs in an annual tax return. Society would merely need to know that people had paid their land rent.

Charging a small land rent for the use of each of the millions of acres of Britain's uplands would free them up and cause a rewilding of Britain. The deforestation brought about by landowners could be reversed.

6.4 Transition

The main problem connected with a transition to the new system is how to move from a thriving economy which is characterised by a very unfair distribution of wealth based on slavery to a thriving economy characterised by a fair distribution of wealth that is based on individual freedom without destroying the economy in the process.

This will be very difficult to achieve, and it is likely to temporarily bring down not only Britain's financial system, but the financial systems of the rest of the world too. Unfortunately, this is the short-term price that has to be paid to get ourselves out of the mess we are in. However, if we work together I think it will bring new meaning to everyone's lives. It will be a way of life in which we would care for each other, collaborate and share instead of selfishly seeking our own wealth at the expense of the slavery of others.

6.4.1 Elements to be transitioned

There are four elements which need to be considered for transition from the old system to the new system: Land, capital, money and debt.

6.4.1.1 Land

The intended ownership of land after transition is clear – it will belong to society. Nobody will be compensated with money for the loss of their freeholds. That includes the foreign owners of land, whose countries may retaliate by annexing any of their land that is owned by British people and organisations.

6.4.1.2 Capital

The basic principle is that wealth, of which capital is a subset, belongs to the people who created it. However, much of the capital created in the past is owned by landowners. Should this be left in hands of the landowners during the transitional period?

Section 2.7 discusses the primary claims on wealth production: land (via rent and subject to the quality of the land), capital (via interest), work (via wages and subject to the merit of the work) and society (via taxes and subject to the level of taxation). Each factor claims its share of the wealth produced, depending on its relative strength. This book has demonstrated that when land is privately owned, it confers an ability on the owner to take more than their fair share of wealth at the expense of the claims of work and society. This is the cause of slavery.

In the new system, land will claim its full share of the wealth it generates for the benefit of society, and taxes will be eliminated. That leaves the two other factors, capital and work, to battle over the remainder.

In the new system, the concept is that because wages are more fairly distributed, the ownership of capital will also be more fairly distributed. However, if after the transition the majority of capital rests in the hands of a minority, the owners of the capital will have the power to take more than their fair share of wealth, at the expense of wages. Having an effective monopoly, these owners of capital will simply charge a high price (in the form of a high interest rate) to anybody who wants to borrow their capital. They will take a larger share of wealth at the expense of wages, and so will defeat the objective of the new system, which is a fair distribution of wealth and an end to slavery.

Therefore it is essential that the transition should address the distribution of capital.

The easiest way is for society to initially take ownership of all significant capital, such as buildings, factories and machinery, and to charge rent for its use. After the transition, people and organisations will be able to buy this capital from society. In addition, any new capital they create will belong to them.

6.4.1.3 Money

The basic principle under the new system is that money belongs to the people who acquired it by selling the wealth they had created. However, in the current system most of the money is owned by landowners and their accomplices. It would perhaps be easiest to stipulate that in the transition all existing money will be cancelled, and a fresh currency will be issued. Each person and organisation in Britain will be issued with a specified amount.

This would of course cause chaos for a while. Leading up to the introduction of the new currency, there would be a hyperinflationary spike in the price of wealth (especially money-equivalent wealth such as gold and silver) as people tried to convert their old currency into wealth. Exchange rates versus foreign currencies would collapse, causing the volume of imported wealth to collapse as well.

6.4.1.4 Debt

The basic principle is that debt certificates rightly belong to the person who loaned their wealth or money to somebody else. However, most of the debt from the past is owned by landowners who have accrued wealth through land ownership. It would perhaps be easiest to stipulate that all debt will be cancelled. So all government debt, mortgage debt, credit card debt, university loan debt, business loans and personal loans would be cancelled.

Debts owed to us from other countries would be cancelled. Likewise, debt that we owe to other countries would be defaulted on.

6.4.2 Transition Strategy

The two choices in relation to a transition are Big Bang or Phased. The Big Bang approach is one in which all the groundwork is done up front, and then there is a sudden switchover. A phased approach is one where the new system would be implemented gradually. It could be phased in over time or perhaps geographically, or possibly in some other way that I haven't thought of.

I suspect there would be little difference between the two in reality. Consider a phased approach where, for example, land rent was slowly increased year by year and current taxes were decreased in the same proportion. As soon as it was realised that land was going to become valueless in a few years, nobody would want to buy it. Why buy something that would soon be worthless? People would start to sell immediately. The price of land would drop very quickly. In 2008, when land prices dropped a tremendous credit crunch started because so much debt and credit was backed by land. The economy crashed. The transitional situation would be very similar to this (and probably much worse for a while) until the economy picked up again under the new system.

6.4.3 Asset-rich, income-poor

People who have spent their life working to pay off a mortgage will not be pleased to find that they no longer own the land they paid for and will have to pay rent for it instead, especially if they are now too old to work to earn the income needed to pay the rent. Measures would be needed to ease the transition for people who are not in a position to work.

7 Conclusion

For the most part, the world has come to accept that people should not be commoditised. They should not be bought and sold in a slave market. What the world has not yet come to accept is that land – the natural resources of the earth – should also not be commoditised, because otherwise the people who depend on them are reduced to becoming slaves of the people who own land, as has been explained in this book.

The biggest benefit of the proposed change towards charging land rent and away from the current system of taxation will be a levelling in human relationships.

I have followed the YouTube vlogs of people who have taken approximately six months to hike the 2,200-mile Appalachian Trail in the USA. During those six months, the hikers all had similar possessions: a backpack containing a tent, a sleeping bag, waterproofs, a spare set of clothes, a small stove, and enough food and water to keep them going for the few days between supply points. Almost without exception, these vloggers have said that this levelling experience restored their faith in human nature. Friendships were easily made, and anybody who was in trouble was helped.

I'd like to think that our society could become more equal, and that we could all enjoy the benefits of improved human relationships. It would be a society in which we would all work collaboratively and collectively, where there was less focus on growth and the economy, and a greater focus on sharing the benefits of the wealth we create.

7 Conclusion

8 Appendices

Bibliography

Ref	Page	
1	1	http://www.oxfam.org.uk/media-centre/press-releases/2016/09/richest-one-percent-owns-twenty-times-more-than-uks-poorest-twenty-percent
2	2	https://www.gov.uk/government/statistics/distribution-of-median-and-mean-income-and-tax-by-age-range-and-gender-2010-to-2011 . Click the link for 2014-5.
3	2	(https://www.gov.uk/government/statistics/investment-income-2010-to-2011). Click the link for 2013-2014
4	2	FOI request to HMRC
5	17	http://www.independent.co.uk/news/business/news/buildings-destroyed-after-rate-relief-is-abolished-892966.html
6	19	https://en.wikipedia.org/wiki/Inclosure_Acts
7	19	http://www.countrylife.co.uk/country-life/who-owns-britain-top-uk-landowners-20178
8	19	http://blogs.ft.com/ftdata/2016/10/24/ft-factcheck-do-we-use-more-land-for-golf-courses-than-we-do-for-homes/
9	21	http://duchyofcornwall.org/london.html
10	22	https://www.gov.uk/government/uploads/system/uploads/attachment_data/file/231599/1434.pdf. Page 6
11	22	https://www.gov.uk/government/uploads/system/uploads/attachment_data/file/231599/1434.pdf. Page 6
12	23	https://www.gov.uk/government/uploads/system/uploads/attachment_data/file/247046/0213.pdf
13	27	http://highpaycentre.org/pubs/10-pay-rise-thatll-do-nicely
14	35	http://www.carlex.org.uk/number-leasehold-homes-double-figure-government-believes-according-leasehold-knowledge-partnership/
15	43	https://www.ons.gov.uk/economy/investmentspensionsandtrusts/bulletins/ownershipofukquotedshares/2015-09-02
16	50	www.gov.uk/government/organisations/rural-payments-agency
17	50	www.cap-payments.defra.gov.uk/download.aspx
18	50	https://www.cchdaily.co.uk/pensions-tax-relief-costs-double-2000
19	50	researchbriefings.files.parliament.uk/.../CDP-2015-0033-Tax-Credits-Key-Statistics.pdf
20	50	https://www.ft.com/content/fa8bd93a-bea1-11e5-9fdb-87b8d15baec2
21	53	https://www.gov.uk/government/organisations/land-registry/about
22	54	https://www.theguardian.com/commentisfree/2014/apr/28/britain-plutocrats-landed-gentry-shotgun-owners)
23	57	https://www.ons.gov.uk/peoplepopulationandcommunity/birthsdeathsandmarriages/lifeexpectancies/bulletins/lifeexpectancyatbirthandatage65bylocalareasinenglandandwales/2015-11-04
24	62	https://www.gov.uk/government/publications/hmrc-annual-report-and-accounts-2015-to-2016/hmrc-annual-report-and-accounts-2015-16-executive-summary
25	68	https://en.wikipedia.org/wiki/Spectrum_auction#United_Kingdom
26	72	http://www.conservativehome.com/highlights/2015/05/lets-not-get-carried-away-the-conservatives-only-won-over-a-quarter-of-all-potential-voters.html
27	78	http://www.lse.ac.uk/genderinstitute/pdf/Confronting-Inequality.pdf Table 2
28	79	http://www.thelondoneconomic.com/news/women-barely-figure-as-part-of-uks-super-rich/27/09/
29	81	researchbriefings.files.parliament.uk/documents/SN05745/SN05745.pdf First column of data in section 2
30	84	http://www.tfa.org.uk/wp-content/uploads/2013/03/TFA2002VisionforAgricultureV7LoRes.pdf. Section 2.2
31	96	https://www.theguardian.com/commentisfree/2014/nov/29/is-it-right-public-schools-charitable-status
32	97	https://www.theguardian.com/education/2015/dec/12/oxford-cambridge-state-school-admissions-failure
33	97	https://www.whatdotheyknow.com/request/landholdings of merton college)
34	97	https://thetab.com/2015/11/12/over-7500-university-staff-are-paid-more-than-100000-a-year-61802
35	99	http://www.suttontrust.com/newsarchive/disturbing-finding-lse-study-social-mobility-britain-lower-advanced-countries-declining/
36	102	http://www.monbiot.com/2017/01/04/the-hills-are-dead.

8 Appendices

Acronyms

GDP	Gross domestic product
HMRC	Her Majesty's Revenue and Customs
MBSS	Modern British Slavery System
UK	United Kingdom of Great Britain and Northern Ireland
VAT	Value Added Tax

22261164R00083

Printed in Great Britain
by Amazon